THE
JESUS NEWSPAPER

The Christian Experiment of 1900
And Its Lessons for Today

Michael Ray Smith

University Press of America,® Inc.
Lanham · New York · Oxford

Copyright © 2002 by
University Press of America,® Inc.
4720 Boston Way
Lanham, Maryland 20706
UPA Acquisitions Department (301) 459-3366

12 Hid's Copse Rd.
Cumnor Hill, Oxford OX2 9JJ

British Library Cataloging in Publication Information Available

06-24-02

ISBN 0-7618-2222-4 (pbk. : alk. paper)

℗™ The paper used in this publication meets the minimum
requirements of American National Standard for Information
Sciences—Permanence of Paper for Printed Library Materials,
ANSI Z39.48—1984

DEDICATION

For My Beloved and Our Beloved

Contents

Foreword

What is the role of journalism today?

Reporting news from a biblical perspective isn't new; it was standard operating procedure in American journalism until 1830 and has been an occasional objective since then. But what does a biblical perspective mean? Staying away from smoking, any kind of drinking, dancing, boxing (as Rev. Charles Sheldon believed) and other personal behaviors deemed wrong? Or does it emphasize more significant personal action plus a way of viewing work and play, politics and economics, literature and the arts, and much else, including journalism itself?

Dr. Michael Smith, journalist and scholar, is well placed to examine these questions. He can teach: He chairs the School of Journalism at Regent University and lectures around the nation. And, unlike many professors, he can write: Over the past two decades numerous columns and articles he has written have appeared in newspapers and magazines such as *USA Today*, *The Atlanta Journal and Constitution*, *World* and *Christianity Today*.

His analysis is especially useful since the post-September-11-2001 days when interest in religious perspectives appears to be growing among journalists and Americans generally. For a time, many reporters looked at publications espousing a religious view only when they had a scandalous televangelist to kick around, or when they might want to crib a story for a Saturday religion section that was largely an excuse for selling ads to churches.

That's all changed now, for five reasons. Let's look first at the most prominent: Sadly, the World War II observation that "There are no atheists in foxholes" is relevant once again. In October 2001 anthrax mailings put journalists on the front lines, and when we're preyed on we tend to pray. Some even ask, "Who is listening to my prayer?" That's when they start regarding journalists who are overt about their religious beliefs not as batty Neanderthals but as people who may have some wisdom.

A second reason is that journalistic baby boomers are aging. Their interests, and those of the boom generation generally, have dominated the news for a third of a century, with college protests in the 1960s, diet books in the 1980s, and Viagra in the 1990s all became big news. Interest in religion generally increases as people age, so it's no surprise that 50-something reporters and their cohort are starting to contemplate God and how He would have us act.

Reason three arises from a new debate about a very old matter: How did things get started? From the 1860s through the 1980s Darwin's theories ruled, opposed only by a tiny, mocked group of creationists. That changed during the 1990s with the advent of "intelligent design" scientists who don't argue from the Bible but instead explain how complicated processes like blood clotting could not have come about through chance mutations. This debate is likely to intensify, and reporters who understand both religion and science will be needed to cover it.

The fourth reason is the rapid explosion of public policy groups in Christianity and Judaism that can speak the language of journalists. For a long time liberal groups coming out of Christianity and Judaism peddled their views but the fundies were stuck in their undies. Now, organizations like the Acton Institute for the Study of Religion and Liberty (where I'm a senior fellow), the Ethics and Public Policy Center, the Institute for Religion and Democracy, and Toward Tradition (an Orthodox Jewish group), have an intellectual sophis-tication that those who tend to sneer cannot overlook.

A fifth reason, more subtle, arises from changes in immigration law that have led to more arrivals from Asia. The number of Hindus in America has increased during the past 30 years from 100,000 to almost a million. The number of Buddhists has similarly climbed. Perhaps six million Muslims now live in the United States, up from about 800,000 three decades ago. Religions that once were exotic in America are now next door, and that raises journalistic and public interest about what those faiths teach.

These five factors and others add up to rapid movement away from what has been called "the naked public square," naked in its lack of religious discussion. What we've learned over the past four decades is that attempts to avoid mentioning religion in public places do not yield neutrality: They leave us naked. The job of journalists, like that of little boys, is to point out when the emperor is naked. But some have been pointing out for a long time that the empire of secularism would eventually fall. Michael Smith shows us the work of one pioneering critic.

Dr. Marvin Olasky
Professor of Journalism,
The University of Texas at Austin,
Senior Fellow, Acton Institute, and
Editor, *World*

Preface

Al Janssen, writer of 22 books, travels the globe talking to writers about the power of the narrative. He knows that the best way to reach a culture that needs a redeemer is to share a gripping story that includes a timeless message that hope follows tragedy. That's the lesson that the Rev. Charles M. Sheldon knew deep within himself, but when he came to the story-telling power of ordinary newspapers, the Congregationalist clergyman abandoned this truth. Too bad. Of all the Christians from all the ages, Sheldon was uniquely positioned to bring about press reform. Nonetheless, his story has the ingredients of a graphic drama. Like a David of old, he took on the Goliath press and slung pebble after pebble its way, but without David's miraculous results. So, what can be learned from an editor who loved to tell stories after the parables of Christ, only to neglect this time-tested technique when he put out a daily newspaper for a week? Plenty.

First, Sheldon put argument over art. Instead of winning his readers over with a story, he gave them sermons. A well-told news story draws readers in. As writer Janssen told a group of wordsmiths, trivial stories told well will get a hearing; profound stories told poorly won't. While Sheldon's poor story telling lost him the call to arms for the Social Gospel, the clergyman-turned-editor made his mark. He did not do it by being excellent as a journalist; he did it by forcing editors and publishers to consider the reader in fresh ways with reader services such as his appeal for famine relief for a starving continent. He provoked hundreds of readers to donate to a worthy cause. Sheldon used his news pages to avert human suffering. Nonetheless, his newspaper missed the opportunity of the age by not rallying for a call to art.

He made advertisers establish policies and drop the convention of publishing nearly any paid announcement that appeared over the transom. But more than anything else, Sheldon did his best to ask that perennial question, "What would Jesus do?" In many ways Sheldon never answered the question with any satisfaction but he made journalists and their audiences wonder about the issue. Furthermore, Sheldon did much to make the press more accountable to readers in a day when screaming headlines ruled the press and the unsung heroes behind the scenes received scant attention in that modest modern enterprise, the production of a daily newspaper.

Dr. Michael R. Smith
Regent University
Virginia Beach

Acknowledgments

Redemption is always a personal matter, and it is the beginning for any task that involves a revolutionary change of view. This book is the result of explorations of a remarkable man who considered redemption the most crucial issue of any age. By examining his work as a journalist, I have come to admire his desire to see the entire world engage Christ in a personal way. While I am indebted to the Rev. Dr. Charles Sheldon for his journalism, I am more indebted to the source of that inspiration, Our Lord, who reminds us in every age of the need to redeem the culture and plant the cross in the socket of the public square.

Others who have inspired me are my wife, Barbara, who has absorbed more journalism than anyone should have to unless it is her business. I acknowledge my children, Shannon and Taylor, both of whom write from the same need that drives all wordsmiths–to recall the passing of the tides with a scrawl that remains just a moment before it is washed to sea. I also thank a team of scholars who ask themselves, "What would Jesus do?" I thank Dr. Dennis E. Hensley, author, educator and trusted confidant, for his relentless editing. I thank Prof. John V. Lawing Jr., resident humorist at Regent University and veteran journalist and editorial cartoonist, for his insights into journalism and publishing in general. I thank Dr. John D. Keeler, scholar and crack copy editor, for his suggestions on macro-considerations and theoretical issues. I thank Dr. J. Douglas Tarpley for his mentoring influence. He is a thinker with the heart of a journalist and an exemplar in his own right. In addition, I thank Dr. Michael Graves for his keen insight in rhetoric, the human condition and genuine faith. I thank colleagues Claire Rundle and Debbie Pope, as well as publishing friend Beverly Baum. Finally, I thank my good friend Cecil Murphey, the consummate author who is as gentle as he is talented.

In addition to the editing friends, I thank my parents, William O. and Ceedie Rae Smith, for their enthusiasm for the mysteries of higher education. I thank my mother for her faith unlike any other that I have ever encountered and my father who taught his family to value learning. No one succeeds unless a cadre of people want that result. That has been the tenor of my family, including my brothers Ronald Smith and Stanley Smith.

For even hereunto were ye called: because Christ also suffered for us, leaving us an example, that ye should follow his steps, 1 Peter 2:21 (KJV).

Chapter 1

What Would Jesus do?

What would Jesus do? That was a popular question during the 1990s as many in the evangelical Christian community found ways to challenge believers to maintain and promote a commitment to Christ using clothing and objects with the letters "WWJD." Most popular were those ubiquitous WWJD bracelets worn by youth and businessmen alike. The bracelets, some woven, some silk-screened, came in a variety of colors from dozens of places and all have the initials "WWJD," short for the question: "What would Jesus do?" (Smith, 1998, p. 17).

This fad began in 1989 when youth leader Janie Tinklenberg designed a bracelet after the then-popular homemade friendship bracelets made of yarn. Tinklenberg wanted to motivate students to ask themselves the question writer Charles Sheldon posed in his best-selling novel *In His Steps* (Smith, 1998, p. 17). In that 1897 work of fiction, a clergyman challenged his congregation to live for one year asking, "What would Jesus do?" when making decisions (Mott, 1947, p. 194).

Where did this question originate? Part of the answer can be found in John P. Ferre's (1988) *A Social Gospel for Millions, the Religious Bestsellers of Charles Sheldon, Charles Gordon, and Harold Bell Wright.*

Ferre found that the question was not original with Sheldon and was part of a stanza in a hymn sung in England before the turn of the century (Ferre, 1988, p. 16). In 1894 William T. Stead described conditions in Chicago in his *If Christ Came to Chicago* published in 1894 by Chicago's Laird and Lee (Mott, 1947, p. 195). Part five of the book was titled "What would Christ do in Chicago?" Sheldon's reliance upon Stead is clear from a concluding passage in Stead's book (Ferre, 1988):

> If Christ came to Chicago what would he wish me to do? That is the question with which I hope every reader will close this book. Nor is the answer difficult or far to seek. For what He would have you do is follow in His footsteps and be a Christ to those among whom you live, in the family, in the workshop, in the city and in the state. (p. 16)[1]

Inspired by Stead, Sheldon went on to write *In His Steps* and influenced a newspaper publisher who asked Sheldon to edit *The Topeka Daily Capital* newspaper for one week in March 1900. Sheldon applied his question "What would Jesus do" to the operation of a general-circulation newspaper during his short tenure as editor, and captivated the nation with the help of an aggressive marketing campaign.

Sheldon tried to apply Christian ideology to news writing, which many readers considered then as now to be philosophically neutral. Sheldon abandoned impartial news reporting and practiced advocacy reporting. He insisted that this Christian approach was superior; however, he failed to appreciate the differences of vastly divergent opinions found in Protestant churches, not the least of which is the proper mode of baptism. With differences of beliefs and practices common in Protestant circles, it was unduly optimistic to think there could be only one type of Christian news. Nonetheless, Sheldon's work captured the popular imagination in the United States. While his novels entertained first and then educated, his newspaper moralized first and failed to entertain. Nonetheless, the experiment was part of a reform movement that helped the country when it faced economic turmoil in the transition from agrarian to industrial enterprises. In addition, it relieved some of the uncertainty among orthodox Christianity on vexing issues such as the believer's role in ushering in Heaven on Earth (Ferre, 1988, p. 8).

Popular culture texts such as newspapers help make these issues transparent (Nelson, 1976, p. 19) and Sheldon's newspaper succeeded

---

[1] *If Christ Came to Chicago*, first published in 1894, can be found in London's *"Review of Reviews"* Office, 1899.

in examining the nature of evil, its source and the nature of good and its ability to resolve conflict. Sheldon's editorials talked frequently of a

Painting photographed by Michael R. Smith at Sheldon's Central Congregational Church in Topeka, Kansas.

The Rev. Dr. Charles M. Sheldon

person's correct relationship with God. These contributions helped to influence the practice of mainstream journalism in the United States; furthermore, his work is important as a case study on defining Christian journalism in the development of the American press.

In the pages ahead, Sheldon's experiment is explored with its attention to evil, manifested in the use of liquor, and the source of good, manifested in individuals who practice the strict morality of Sheldon's code. Sheldon's use of formulas are examined as part of his definition of Christian journalism. These issues are explored with particular attention to Sheldon's six editorials. *The Jesus Newspaper* provides some insight into a person's attempt at creating an ideologically driven newspaper committed to Christian evangelism and meant for a general audience. Sheldon shared the gospel message in his editorials and this aspect alone makes the content Christian, but its lack of news coverage made it a poor substitute for a vigorous newspaper. Critics of the day called the experiment a failure, but they may have been too hard on a pioneer who has since made his mark in journalism. The following chapters examine Sheldon's newspaper work for its lessons regarding newspaper publishing, its value to those interested in wedding ideology to journalistic efforts, and its general historical value.

Research is often autobiographic and historian Marsden suggests that scholars reveal their point of view for readers to consider (1994, p. 7). Here are some of mine. I possess firsthand experience as a journalist for more than 20 years. Nearly a decade of that time was spent working full-time in a variety of newsrooms: a semi-weekly publication of *The News-Chronicle* in central Pennsylvania, a Gannett-owned daily in Chambersburg, *Lancaster Newspapers,* Lancaster and *The Sunday Grit* in Williamsport, all in Pennsylvania and *The Atlanta Journal-Constitution* and several other community newspapers. It has been my privilege to evaluate newspapers and magazines for national contests. This professional background informs my work along with my personal faith. As a Protestant Christian, I subscribe to orthodox Christianity with emphasis on salvation through faith in Christ. In addition to my professional work and personal faith, my identity has been shaped by a public school education in suburban Washington, D.C., in a middle-class neighborhood of single-family houses. I agree with Geertz, who said that " . . . man is an animal suspended in webs of significance he himself has spun. I take culture to be those webs, and the analysis of it to be therefore not an experimental science in search of law but an interpretive one in search of meaning" (1995, p. 5).

Disclosure notwithstanding, this research attempts to avoid the tendency of revisionist historians who "reinterpret past events according to contemporary concerns, seeing history through the lens of feminism, multiculturalism, and post-Marxist politics" (Veith, 1994, p. 99). Christianity cannot be dismissed in understanding the press of America, and more research of the press of yesteryear will help scholars understand the press of today. Sloan (1991) warned of interpretation of historic evidence that leads to distortion; however, interpretation can provide the explanation of the past that will provide insight into the world of today.

This study arises from interest in the Rev. Dr. Charles M. Sheldon's attempt to make a mainstream, daily newspaper a Christian newspaper, and this research attempts to interpret Sheldon's work as a newspaper editor for a week with *The Topeka Daily Capital.* Throughout this study, the newspaper that Sheldon edited will be called by its name of the day, The Jesus Newspaper. It also was known as Sheldon's Newspaper or the Ideal Newspaper. All the phrases refer to the same six issues *of The Topeka Daily Capital* published from March 13 to March 17, 1900.

The study begins with a chapter stating the background of Sheldon's newspaper experiment. In addition, it explores the "What would Jesus do?" question. Chapter two discusses Sheldon's writing career and Chapter three examines the linkage between Christianity and journalism. Chapter four explores the role of Sheldon's newspaper experiment during his day. Chapter five examines the culture of society in 1900. Chapter six looks at the culture of newspapers during this period, and chapter seven examines the culture of Christian journalism in the late nineteenth century. These chapters provide the cultural context and background for the Sheldon experiment. Chapter eight examines this newspaper in detail and offers an analysis. Chapter nine offers some conclusions based on the experiment.

The last section of this study concludes with an appendix that re-prints the exact words of the editorials, as they appeared when Sheldon was editor of *The Topeka Daily Capital.*

Chapter 2

Sheldon's Writing Career Before The Jesus Experience

In Toynbee's (1956) examination of civilization, he refers to Christianity with high regard; however, because of the faith's exclusive claim, he stopped short of an all-out endorsement. In an earlier study of 21 world civilizations in the 1940s, he (1948) learned that societies disintegrate because of a decay of the soul (Waugh, 1992). Toynbee's work suggested the crucial role religion plays in the health of a culture, including religious systems. From Socrates until French philosopher Auguste Comte, the idea of a personal God was an accepted part of the terrain for residents of the West. With Comte's logical positivism and empiricism, acceptance of a personal God was pushed to the background, neither forgotten nor discarded-just detached by many people as the primary cause for most of this life's unfolding.

The Renaissance served as a catalyst that broke the spell of the Middle Ages, and science appeared ready to explain all of life's mysteries. Order and rationality replaced the idea of a Creator who controlled the universe. The Enlightenment compared the world to a machine, with God acting as the absentee operator; the Romantics opposed this metaphor, preferring to see God intimately associated with nature as part of the life force that surges, pulses, and throbs throughout the wild. With each philosophical movement, the idea of a personal God faded another shade like a black-and-white photograph that was developed but not allowed to stand in a fixing agent long enough before light obliterates the image.

In the development of American journalism, Christianity has played a role and changed from a dominant position in the seventeenth century to a marginal position in the late twentieth century (Nord, 1990; Olasky, 1988). Where once the press in the United States organized its content around a Christian perspective, the idea of Christian journalism became a novelty, in part because it is difficult to define.

As early as 1895 Sheldon began his crusade to reinstate Christianity into a newspaper (Ripley, 1965, p. 7). By April of that year, Sheldon preached about the idea, saying, "A Christian daily would have to be a real newspaper. It could not be conducted on any namby pamby, goody goody basis" (Miller, 1987, p. 105). Much has been written about Sheldon and his work with scholars such as Woodworth (1983) examining the remarkable clergyman's life. Others explored the newspaper project, but no one has looked deeply at the Sheldon blueprint before the experiment or discussed at length the role of his novels in formulating the newspaper plan. Finally, researchers have not explored these elements and then applied rhetoric theory to The Jesus Newspaper.[2] In many ways Sheldon did everything anyone could do to explain his vision in the abstract. He used sermons to outline the idea and published his plans in the *Kingdom*, a Social Gospel weekly published in Minneapolis, yet he still found the sting of misunderstanding as soon as his newspaper hit the streets across the nation and in London.

Sheldon's experiment to transform a mainstream, general circulation newspaper into a Christian daily was meant for a heterogeneous audience, an idea that was tried before but with little success. Scholars know much of Sheldon, but his newspaper artifact remains largely unexplored. Woodworth (1983) did not make an in-depth analysis of the text of Sheldon's editorials as a rhetorical artifact nor did he examine the assumptions of the Sheldon model of Christian journalism. This research explores the news, editorials and other parts of the newspaper with particular attention to the need for story telling to remain paramount whenever a deep truth is present.

The purpose of this research is to examine Sheldon's example of Christian journalism, using rhetorical criticism. The goal is to explore the Sheldon model of integration of Christianity and journalism. In this examination of Sheldon's work, primarily his editorials, the focus will be on exploring Charles Sheldon's idea of organizing a mainstream

---

[2] The phrase "The Jesus Newspaper," when not italicized refers to the Sheldon newspaper. *The Jesus Newspaper*, when italicized, refers to this book.

general circulation newspaper around Christianity. In addition, *The Jesus Newspaper* examines the ways the Rev. Dr. Charles M. Sheldon defined Christian journalism. Sheldon's work as editor of *The Topeka Daily Capital* in March 1900 suggested a definition of Christian journalism. For this study, Christian journalism is operationally defined as journalism produced by a Christian to support the assumptions of Christian ideology. In other words, in his role as news gatherer, the journalist gathers news that contributes to Christian values and selects news that serves the interests of Christianity. On the other hand, religious journalism is defined in this study as articles pertaining to religion, just another function of news gathering.

Sheldon's Writing Career

To gain an appreciation for Sheldon and his approach to Christian journalism, it is useful to briefly examine Sheldon's writing career and summarize the events surrounding his remarkable experiment. Sheldon began his writing career penning melodramatic novels from his sermon series designed to attract students from Washburn College in Topeka, Kansas. In 1890, Sheldon began his first series (Mott, 1947, p. 194). In 1894, the *Chicago Advance*, a Congregational weekly began printing the fiction as a series and A.C. McClurg and Company of Chicago released the series as a book with the title *The Crucifixion of Philip Strong*. In 1896 the Congregational Sunday School and Publishing Society of Boston issued another novel by Sheldon. In 1897 the Advance published Sheldon's most famous novel, *In His Steps*, subtitled *What Would Jesus Do?* By 1899 the Advance Publishing Company produced four editions of *In His Steps* in 10 cent-, 25 cent-, 45 cent-, and 75 cent-editions as well as illustrated $1.25 edition. Although the Advance Publishing Company obtained a proper copyright on its book, the Advance periodical did not have a proper copyright. By 1947 as many as eighteen American book publishers took advantage of the faulty copyright and released their own versions of *In His Steps*, treating it as material in the public domain (p. 195). Although Sheldon estimated that his novel sold more than thirty million copies and Baker Book House estimated more than twenty-two million copies were sold (Sheldon, 1994, p. 7), Mott (1947) estimated that number to be closer to two million (p. 197).

Regardless of the number of copies sold, the novel made Sheldon, a shy man, a sensation because of its new approach to combating social ills. He captured readers' attention with the question, "What would Jesus do?" Sheldon was not alone in this endeavor. During this period a new breed of American clergy was engaged in trying to remedy the social problems of the poor, particularly in cities. This era was the decade of William and Catherine Booth and their Salvation Army. During the 1890s Humphrey Ward's novel *Robert Elsmere* also challenged Christians to infiltrate the slums to redeem its denizens (p. 194). However, it was Sheldon's novel that inspired an experiment in journalism that came to be known as the newspaper that Jesus edited.

Sheldon had lectured about the idea of a Christian daily newspaper throughout 1895 and wrote about the concept for *The Kingdom* in Minneapolis, Minnesota, on June 28 and July 5, 1895, and *The Topeka Daily Capital* April 23, 1895 (Ripley, 1965, p. 7). In 1896 Arthur Capper was part owner and publisher of the *Topeka Mail and Breeze* (Woodworth, 1983, p. 97). On July 2, 1896 a crowd of prominent Topeka citizens gathered at a midweek service at Topeka's Central Church. Among those in the audience was Capper who posed questions on living the Christian life (p. 112). At that meeting it was Capper who asked Sheldon for suggestions for publishers of mainstream newspapers who "desire of doing all within their power in the interest of Christianity and good morals" (Ripley, 1968, p. 247). Sheldon told the audience that he suggested the publishers identify their newspapers as non-political, insist on bylines for all news articles and avoid any content that was impure. On July 10, 1896, Capper told his readers in his *Topeka Mail and Breeze* that a newspaper such as the one outlines by Sheldon could not be profitable.

However, by 1899 Sheldon had refined his vision of a Christian daily newspaper in an interview with George T. B. Davis of *Our Day*. He insisted that the ideal newspaper employ only Christians as newsgatherers and publish news of religion from around the world along with fiction like the serials he used in his Congregationalist pulpit that were then published as melodramatic novels (Woodworth, 1983, p. 127). Sheldon told Davis that the enterprise would cost one million dollars and would be best suited for a metropolitan area of 50,000 to 100,000 residents, not a town the size of Topeka that possessed 30,000 people in 1900.

Nonetheless, by 1900 the vision had become a reality when Frederick O. Popenoe, principal owner of Topeka's only morning newspaper, *The Topeka Daily Capital,* suggested that Sheldon attempt the experiment. Sheldon's novel, *In His Steps,* gave a blueprint for his Christian daily newspaper as part of the fictional narrative. As editor, Sheldon implemented many of the policies and initiatives that his fictional editor, Edward Norman of the *Daily News,* put into practice in the mythical city of Raymond.

Ripley (1965) said Sheldon accepted Popenoe's offer "to demonstrate to the public in general and to the skeptical American press in particular the practicability of publishing a simon-pure daily as he thought Jesus would. The result was a paper that has come to be known variously as the Sheldon edition, the Christian daily, and Sheldon's ideal paper" (p. 2). However, Ripley missed a deeper issue, that this study examines the way Sheldon defined Christian journalism.

Early in his ministry in Topeka, Sheldon studied eight occupations including the business of journalism and spent a week working as a reporter for *The Topeka Daily Capital* (Woodworth, 1983, p. 113). That week as a reporter taught Sheldon several lessons (Sheldon, 1890, pp. 372-373). Among the lessons for Sheldon was that as powerful as the press was, it did not understand news in light of eternity. However, newspapers influenced working people. To Sheldon, a devout Christian, the greatest need in the United States at that time was to establish a Christian newspaper to reach the nation, particularly ordinary working-class Americans.

An ordained Congregational minister, Sheldon's early brush with journalism had an impact on his ministerial career. He was the son of a New York farmer and Congregational minister (Sheldon, 1925, p. x), and graduated from Brown University in 1883 and Andover Theological Seminary in 1886. He began his ministry as pastor of a Congregational Church in Waterbury, Vermont, in 1886. He was pastor of a Central Congregational Church in Topeka, Kansas, from 1889 to 1912. There he wrote thirty fictional narratives and read them to his congregation. Between 1896 and 1897 he wrote *In His Steps*, and read it in installments on Sunday evenings to his congregation. After his success as editor of *The Topeka Daily Capital* in March 1900, Sheldon traveled to Great Britain, Australia, New Zealand and France to lobby for Prohibition, one of his pet issues while editor of *The Topeka Daily Capital*. From 1920 to 1924 Sheldon was editor-in-chief of the *Christian Herald* in New York. He edited the *Everyday Bible* in 1924 and spent his remaining years speaking and writing (p. xi). By the time Sheldon died in 1946, Prohibition had passed from the law of the land. It was national law in 1920; however, in 1933 it was repealed because it was thought to contribute to, rather than reduce, crime.

Interest in and Promotion of the Experiment

It was December 29, 1899, only 13 years after Sheldon began his ministry, that Popenoe arranged for Sheldon to edit *The Topeka Daily Capital* for six issues from March 13 to March 17, 1900. Sheldon agreed, stipulating that his share of the profits, $5,000, should be destined for philanthropic purposes (Sheldon, 1925, p. 139). *In His Steps*, subtitled *What Would Jesus Do?*, suggested ways Christ would behave if he had worked in various occupations, including journalism.

The combination of the novel's fame and Popenoe's aggressive promotion of the Sheldon edition ensured widespread attention and the formation of a community intent on observing the experiment. The newspaper printed sermons on the front page and average daily circulation soared to 362,684, with orders coming from overseas. In 1887, Joseph Pulitzer's *New York World* had a circulation of 190,000 during the week and a quarter of a million on Sunday (Stephens, 1997, p. 200). Both the *World* and the *New York Journal* broke circulation records following the McKinley-Bryan election and each sold approximately 1.5 million newspapers (Emery, Emery and Roberts, 1996, p. 200).

The novel concerned the ministry of the Rev. Henry Maxwell of First Church who encountered vagrant Jack Manning. Out of work and seeking some help, Manning attended one of Maxwell's services and scolded the congregation for not acting on its faith. Following the tramp's collapse and later death, Maxwell challenged his congregation to make decisions based on the concept: What would Jesus do? The first church member to respond to the challenge was Edward Norman, editor of the *Raymond Daily News*, who reversed years of newspaper tradition by not publishing news that he thought Jesus would find objectionable. For instance, Norman told his managing editor not to print a sports article about the victory of a popular fighter. In addition, Norman altered the newspaper's advertising policy and stopped its Sunday publication. While these changes hurt business, Norman found fulfillment in behaving as he thought Jesus would behave in the same situation. Ultimately, an heiress was forced to use her personal fortune to salvage the failing publication. In the novel, the success of Norman's newspaper inspired others to found similar newspapers across the nation.

Critics scorn Sheldon's novel as inferior fiction (Mott, 1947, p. 195) lacking in literary style and plausibility of plot (Ripley, 1965, p. 3); yet Sheldon's "What would Jesus do?" question made faith a matter of social responsibility and intrigued readers. They mused on the notion that every aspect of life could be redeemed, including a daily newspaper. Aware of this popularity, Popenoe approached Sheldon at a party on November 3, 1899, and made him a proposition. Popenoe offered Sheldon an experiment, to edit his newspaper for one week according to the principles Jesus might use (Sheldon, 1925, p. 113).

While Popenoe presented the experiment as a test for mainstream newspapers, his ultimate motivation was to capitalize on Sheldon's popularity to make a sudden financial windfall. No journalist himself, Popenoe was a wealthy businessman. In July 1899 he formed a corporation to buy *The Topeka Daily Capital* from the Bank of Topeka (Ripley, 1965, p. 6). The Bank of Topeka acquired the newspaper from its founder, Joseph K. Hudson, in 1895 when Hudson became financially overextended in real estate dealings. Popenoe paid just 10% down on a $50,000 debt to purchase *The Topeka Daily Capital,* the only morning newspaper in the city. David Mulvanae, the banker at the Bank of Topeka and a Republican, insisted that Hudson be the editor, assuring that *The Topeka Daily Capital* would remain stridently Republican. To make room for Hudson, editor Harold T. Chase was demoted to associate editor. Popenoe controlled 51% of the newspaper stock; business manager Dell Keizer, Hudson's son-in-law, controlled 20%; editor Harold T. Chase controlled 17% with the remaining 12% spread out among several of Popenoe's associates.

Although Chase and Keizer opposed the idea of the experiment, Popenoe was enthusiastic and he controlled the newspaper. During July 1899 when Popenoe made his offer to Sheldon, Sheldon spoke at the Eighteenth International Christian Endeavor Convention in Detroit, and urged someone among the four million members to attempt a Christian newspaper. Sheldon said the project would cost a million dollars (Ripley, 1965, pp. 8-9). During his speeches, Sheldon predicted that a newspaper like the one Edward Norman edited in Sheldon's novel would be a reality. Popenoe capitalized on this built-in support and hired Auguste C. Babize to handle the public relations. Babize was a well-known reporter for the *Chicago Times-Herald* and wrote a dispatch about the coming Sheldon experiment for the Associated Press wire service; however, he also was working clandestinely for Popenoe as his secret press agent (p. 10). Even in 1900 this arrangement was no less than a major conflict of interest. Nonetheless, Babize wrote the first announcement of the experiment Monday, January 22, 1900, urging readers to subscribe to the Sheldon edition of *The Topeka Daily Capital* during the week of March 13, 1900. "The announcement of the Sheldon edition made the front pages of many Western and Midwestern dailies," wrote Ripley (1965, p. 10). Readers familiar with the plot of *In His Steps* and the business reversals of editor Edward Norman speculated on how Sheldon would fare against his fictional counterpart. *The Topeka Daily Capital,* which did not publish on Mondays, published the news of the Sheldon experiment across its front page Tuesday, January 23, 1900. Babize had extra copies of this edition sent to influential people across the United States. In addition, he had editor Hudson write a letter that was sent to every clergyman in Kansas inviting him to express an opinion in advance of the experiment. For his part, Babize was promised stock in *The Topeka Daily Capital* and a job as a managing editor following the experiment (p. 12).

Babize then hired his friend Herbert S. Houston, a news reporter-turned-advertising sales manager, for New York City's *Outing Magazine* to handle all of *The Topeka Daily Capital*'s non-local advertising (Sheldon, 1925, p. 121). A Kansas native, Houston was well acquainted with the Sheldon legend and he did much to sell advertising and promote circulation. Both men worked together to obtain national subscriptions and targeted the 55,000 societies of the interdenominational "Christian Endeavor." Organized from 1900 to 1915, the Christian Endeavor was a youth organization of 30 Protestant denominations on the order of today's Youth for Christ organization. Houston convinced the publisher of the *Christian Endeavor World* to donate the back page of the February 8, 1900, issue to announce the experiment (Houston, 1936, pp. 15-16). The *Christian Herald* did not advertise the experiment but helped by sharing its 16,000-subscriber mailing list with *The Topeka Daily Capital*. Gilson Willetts, a free-lance reporter for the *Christian Herald*, wrote a series of articles preceding the Sheldon experiment and each article ended with a suggestion by Willett's editor that *Christian Herald* readers should subscribe to the Sheldon edition. Other publications such as *Epworth Herald* and the *Baptist Young People's Union* helped with the promotion effort.

The efforts of Babize and Houston led to a circulation bonanza. During the week in which Sheldon worked as editor, circulation went from 11,223 newspapers on week days, and 12,298, Sundays, to an average of 362,684 copies each day (p. 13). To meet the publishing demands, the *Capital* ran its press non-stop producing 120,000 a day. In addition, the *Chicago Journal*, the *Staats Zeitung* German-language newspaper in New York City and the *Westmister Gazette* in London printed the newspaper (Miller, 1987, p. 111). However, the experiment would not have attracted this many readers without the aggressive national promotion; it would have remained a local phenomenon. Nonetheless, the large audience constituted a community that will be important to consider in later chapters when the idea of sharing a common vision is discussed.

During the experiment, Popenoe raised the news stand price of the newspaper from 10 cents to 25 cents per copy and increased the advertising rate and eventually made more than $20,000 for the one week of news distribution. Advertisers were anxious to be included in the experiment, but Sheldon rejected objectionable display advertisements, even ones from loyal advertisers in *The Topeka Daily*

Capital (Sheldon, 1925, pp. 121-122). Sheldon banned tobacco, patent medicines, bargain sales, corsets, illustrations of ladies's hosiery and underwear, theater and sporting events and advertisements from the large department stores in Kansas City. Hudson worried that Sheldon would embarrass the newspaper, and business manager Dell Keizer predicted lawsuits if Sheldon pulled advertisements from existing sales contracts. To protect against those contingencies, Popenoe had a contract developed that leased the Capital Publishing Company and the newspaper operation to Sheldon for one week. Attorney Sam Gardenshire, a copyright lawyer in New York City, advised Popenoe to draft an agreement by which the physical properties of the *Captial* Publishing Company and its Associated Press franchise were leased to Sheldon. However, Sheldon did not realize that the contract held him responsible for any lawsuits that erupted even though no one ever sued. Sheldon did not comment on the lease in his autobiography.

Following the success of Sheldon's experiment, Popenoe planned to continue to publish *The Topeka Daily Capital* as a Christian daily newspaper with Babize as managing editor ("A big row is on," 1900, p. 1). However, Keizer and Chase challenged the plan and soon it was abandoned. Within a year Popenoe lost control of *The Topeka Daily Capital* to Arthur Capper, a journalist trained by Hudson.[3] Popenoe used his $20,000 profits from the Sheldon experiment in an attempt to sustain the artificial circulation that was created by the experiment but defaulted on his bank loan and lost his investment in *The Topeka Daily Capital* (Ripley, 1965, p. 36). Popenoe moved to Costa Rica and worked in mining, then moved to southern California and established a nursery for subtropical fruits, introducing the Fuerte avocado and Deglet Noor dates to the state.

After Popenoe defaulted on his loan, Keiser and Hudson left *The Topeka Daily Capital* and organized the *Daily Herald*, a Republican newspaper published from July 1901 to July 1907 (p. 39). Babize went on to study law, founded Investment Services Company and later wrote that the Sheldon experiment was his idea (Babize, 1935, p. 73).

---

[3] Capper proved his ability in publishing and produced a monthly in 1900, *Missouri Valley Farmer*. He went on to acquire a number of publications and two radio stations following his success as governor of Kansas, 1915-1919. Later his publishing empire became known as Stauffer Publications' Home State Farm Publications with a combined circulation of more than one million.

Chapter 3

The Link Between Christianity and Journalism

The Sheldon edition is of interest to scholars because it provides another look at the journalism of 1900. Although the newspaper was a novelty, it represents one person's attempt to reform the press in the throes of sensationalism. Sheldon attempted to practice advocacy journalism, but he wanted to present his news as no different than other mainstream efforts. This unusual approach makes Sheldon's work worth studying. As an outsider to journalism, Sheldon thought he could bring a pristine vision to the conventional practices. His use of Christianity as a way to reform and reshape the press provides another reason to examine his efforts.

Sheldon approached journalism in the way that reformed Christian George M. Marsden (1994) tracked the study of knowledge in the United States. Marsden noted in his *The Soul of the American University* that Protestant thinking dominated late nineteenth century culture, forming the basis for academic education. Within this period, liberal Protestantism stood for inclusiveness and tolerance for religious diversity. This tolerance, however, contributed to the weakening of religious convictions, as Protestantism became a homogenized blend of ideas. This inclusiveness, seen most visibly in the 1880s, permitted even secular thinking to gain equal standing with religious ideas. Ultimately, science gained dominance over religion in its ability to provide explanations for life. Marsden says that in the 1880s, when

Yale's William G. Sumner received permission to use a text from agnostic Herbert Spencer, religion was considered fading in its influence.

Weber (1930) noted that Protestantism is particularly suited to integrating itself into the secular part of society, which allows it to compete with "the meaning systems of rationalism" (Hoover, 1989, p. 41). Hoover described the dualistic role of religion in society, sometimes public, sometimes private called this process "the democratization of American Christianity" (p. 7) and noted that Protestantism used media to establish religion as a basis for influence in the public realm, while insisting that it was part of the private realm of life in society. Neuhaus (1984) took a different view, saying that the secular doctrines of the eighteenth century developed to avoid the religion-inspired wars of Europe. He argued that this notion became the basis of the U.S. Constitution. However, Neuhaus went on to write about the need for Christians to express their faith in the public sphere:

> . . . Christians nonetheless find themselves within the compromised orders of the world. Because they believe that Christian truth is not private truth but is public truth, there is the irrepressibly felt need to relate that truth to the several worlds in which we are involved. (p. 119)

As the press developed in the United States after World War I and formalized its conventions, journalists adopted the objectivity notion as the standard (Schudson, 1978). In the contemporary period of the press that Sloan (1991) dates from 1945 until today, reporters have become comfortable with articles that reflect a political convention, found as early as 1765 with party press newspapers, but not religion. Today only writers designated as religion reporters are expected to cover religion news and the expectation is that their articles will often refer to the sterile operation of an institution and its misfeasance or malfeasance. Reports on theological questions are considered part of the routine when accompanied by enough controversy to warrant the examination. Questions about life and meaning are rarely tackled and are only presented in a specialized department known as religion, making religion news a ghetto within the mainstream press.

When religion breaks through the departmentalization of the newspaper and appears in a prominent place such as page one, the characterization is sometime fraught with the tragic, heroic or threatening frames used to organize important news. In 1993, when *Washington Post* reporter Michael Weisskopf wrote that religious conservatives were largely poor, uneducated and easy to command, three editors reviewed that line but failed to question it. *The Washington Post*'s David Broder, well known for his political commentary, said the problem with the *Post* editors was that they did not know any evangelicals; they were outside their sphere of influence.

Part of the reason newspapers are struggling with the proper frame in which to discuss groups with religious associations is the problem frequently identified by surveys: professional self-selection (Lichter, Lichter, Rothman, 1986). Reporters tend to be culled from a similar cultural, social and economic class that promotes a similar value system. This observation by itself does not explain the reason religion is not covered with the same intensity as most other departments in the standard newspaper. Buddenbaum (1987) studied religion news coverage in three large dailies and found that writers tended to write in-depth stories, a trend that she traces to the 1970s. In addition, she found that the daily newspapers she studied would occasionally publish religion stories "in the regular news columns" (p. 601). While her research provided some verification that the religion coverage assignments were as respectable as other assignments, questions about a Christian perspective as a news standard have remained illusive.

While this book is not a study of the present-day approach of journalists to the definition of Christian journalism, it is important to remember that the issue is of relevance as a research area for the press of any era. This research examines Sheldon's work as an editor of a mainstream, daily newspaper to better understand his definition of Christian journalism in 1900. This definition has changed since the founding of the nation. In colonial America, the press reflected great reverence for spiritual issues and spoke of Providence routinely in news content. For those working in the colonial press the problem was not tension over the content of the newspaper, but supplies to print. Cressy (1987) found that the challenges of obtaining paper, presses and the other materials needed to publish in the late 1700s were great. However, Emery et al (1996) considered these and other obstacles as evidence that the colonists could overcome adversity out of a conviction that they were the chosen ones of God. Akin to the idea that the Puritans had about a divine mandate to possess New England, the Emery interpretation suggested that America was divinely destined to succeed through its savior, the indomitable press, and the cleansing power of democracy.

Emery et al (1996) wrote that English religious dissenters settled New England, and the colonies reflected the religious and political troubles of Europe. But Cressy noted that religion was but one of a multitude of factors that drove migration across the ocean to New England. Cressy (1987) characterized the Pilgrim story as over-emphasizing the religious overtones, saying that this version was useful to the Puritan religious defenders in the 1670s to control the "rising generations" (p. 76). He wrote that the "religion-drove-migration" explanation "is not good history." The religion-as-motivation explanation is so widespread, said Cressy, because of the high number of clergymen who wrote history, but with only partial information.

Nonetheless, Hart (1990) challenged the Cressy view. Hart noted that the Pilgrims who settled at Plymouth Rock in 1620 were members of the Congregational Church who separated themselves from the Church of England out of belief that the truth consisted of a voluntary fellowship. Hart went on to reason that Pilgrims only considered truth that was not imposed by government or the Church of England. King James I, the head of the Church of England, persecuted the Congregationalists for their separatist views, forcing the separatists to flee first to Holland, then to what became Cape Cod, Massachusetts. When the Mayflower and the forty members of the Separatist church arrived at Cape Cod, the pastor of the congregation, John Robinson, drafted the Mayflower Compact. It said the community would recognize just and equal law for all, including the other sixty-two passengers on the ship who were not members of the Congregationalist Church (pp. 67-74).

Historians continue to debate the intensity of the religious motivation that prompted the immigration to the colonies, yet it is clear that the press of the period was marked by a strong Christian flavor. More will be said on this issue in chapter seven; but suffice it to say that newspapers in other regions of the nation printed content that read like sermons during the 1730s. In addition to Nord (1990), Williams (1994) found that the *South-Carolina Gazette* spoke of sin, conversion and regular church attendance. The goal of this newspaper, founded by Benjamin Franklin and Thomas Whitmarsh, was to assist in the overall good of society. Religious publications are still available today, but mainstream newspapers, by definition, are secular and non-sectarian, although they insist their goal is to promote the public good by disseminating information that will help readers make good decisions. This study does not argue that Christianity has lost its privileged position in American journalism; instead the book explores one person's attempt to practice Christian journalism and what it meant then and now. That man, Sheldon, was a Protestant pastor who thought the idea was possible. In the chapters ahead, the era in which Sheldon lived and worked, and the secular and the sectarian press of his day, is examined to gain insight into the culture that influenced his definition of Christian journalism.

Summary

While journalism and Christianity were firmly linked in the colonies, the two tended to separate as the nation matured. With this came changes in the way journalism was defined. The purpose of this research is to examine Sheldon's example of Christian journalism, using a type of rhetorical criticism known as symbolic convergence theory. In this examination of Sheldon's work, primarily his editorials, the research question is: On the basis of Charles Sheldon's work as a newspaper editor for one week in a mainstream general circulation newspaper, how did he define Christian journalism? Sheldon's novel, *In His Steps,* is used to gain insight into Sheldon's ideas on journalism from the approach used by the fictional editor who tried to make the content of his general-circulation newspaper conform to the kind of press Jesus would practice.

Chapter 4

Approaching The Jesus Newspaper

How do we define history? Since this work uses an historical approach and methodology, it is important to define some concepts. Cairns defined history "as the interpreted literary reconstruction of the socially significant human past, based on data from documents studied by scientific methods" (1979, p. 15). His paradigm leans toward information rather than interpretation or criticism; however, he is not content with exclusive approaches such as examining the event alone, or artifacts extant from the event, but encourages an analysis of the artifact or event to gain understanding of its meaning. Herodotus linked *histria* to inquiry and this Latin word became "history" for English speakers (p. 14). The Apostle Paul used a form of this word, *historesai,* in Galatians 1:18 to mean "to investigate, to obtain firsthand information."

In addition, Cairns wrote that history could include the interpretation of past space-time events (p. 14) or the imaginative importation of the results of research as in a literary work (p. 15). This research on Sheldon and his newspaper experiment refers to all these areas by examining the culture in which Sheldon lived and worked, the novel that outlined in fictional form the experiment that Sheldon actually conducted with the literal newspaper content that he produced in his week as editor.

Historic research can be organized into three approaches: ideological, professional and cultural (Sloan, 1991). The ideological approach says historians write from their own ideological perspective in interpreting the facts. For instance, in the eighteenth century, nationalist historians reflected their own deep patriotism and talked of humankind's developing liberty. Influenced by the Enlightenment, which said rational laws govern nature (Veith, 1994), these historians tended to side with the established order. Romantics followed by emphasizing the role of great men; their accounts read like literature. The Progressive School was a reaction to the nationalist and romantic approaches by emphasizing ideological conflict between a press seeking liberty and freedom, and the forces of wealth and power (1991). This school led to the development of the Consensus interpretation, which argued that agreement, not conflict, marked history; belief in democracy and freedom helped the press work with institutions, such as government, to improve life.

Because many journalism historians worked first in the mass media, their professional backgrounds influenced their historiography. The professional perspective takes a developmental approach and examines the development of proper practices and outlooks in journalism as a profession and industry (1991). For instance, in 1873 Frederic Hudson considered Benjamin Day's *New York Sun* (begun in 1833) to be the proper kind of journalism because it made an inexpensive newspaper available to everyone (Sloan, 1991). The Developmental School took the position that the professional standards that developed over time were the appropriate ones, but it went on to emphasize the role of the press to confront other institutions to achieve change (1991).

The cultural perspective says that impersonal social forces should be the focus in historical investigations; media are linked to their environment and sociological forces, and economics and technology interrelate with media (1991). In 1925 urban sociologist Robert E. Park of the University of Chicago wrote in his *The Natural History of the Newspaper*, "that the evolution of American journalism resulted from its interaction with surrounding culture" (Sloan, 1991, p. 8). The cultural view is more concerned with the impact society has on the media rather than the media's impact on society. Cairns suggested this kind of approach with the study of an incident or the study of indirect information such as records (p. 12).

Tarpley's "Anne O'Hare McCormick" (1984) is an example of a blended approach to writing history. It suggested an ideological approach by presenting McCormick as the pioneering woman who opened up the field for other women opinion writers. In addition, it showed the development of normative values, such as the use of a notepad as part of the convention in the role of reporter source and the power issues involved in an interview, the controlled conversation. And, finally, the piece suggested the cultural perspective in that McCormick was discussed in terms of the influence of her childhood at volatile places around the world as the kind of preparation that would serve her well when she covered news and newsmakers as an adult.

When Carey talked of the relationship of media to human consciousness, he talked of the cultural perspective. Journalism historians who have used this approach have used the term "symbolic–meaning" to describe this philosophical and sociological approach (Sloan, 1991). Covert (1981) and Henry (1976) offer approaches that explore under-represented figures from the past. In addition, Nerone's idea (1987) of examining the community press helps scholars understand the press in mainstream measures that are missing when too much attention is lavished on urban centers such as New York City.

Regardless of the system for organizing the various approaches to history, a question of the relevance of this pursuit confronts students and educators of media history. Beasley and Ward (1993) noted that a study of journalism history was once considered crucial to understand the "democratic decision-making" of the representative form of government, whereas newspapers were thought to be the instrument whereby active readers became informed and could engage in the process of influencing elected leaders (p. 13). The flaw with this idea was that historians wrote as if the notion of democracy, a noble ideal, was a given and history supported gradual but inevitable progress. Startt characterizes this approach as projecting the present back into the past, or the "Whig fallacy" after Herbert Butterfield's Whig Interpretation of History (1931, p. 21).

Startt (1993) noted the field of historiography went through a period of ideological consensus during the 1930s through 1950s when mass media was thought to be very powerful in modeling public opinion. With the 1960s, historians reflected the "rebellion against authority" and challenged the fundamental assumptions of doing history, including the idea that objectivity was possible (Startt, pp. 22-23). More recently, the field has fragmented into sub fields to identify the oppression associated with African-Americans, women and other groups considered by some to be disenfranchised and neglected by historians using the orthodox approach.

In short, history is crucial in scholarship, and research of a figure such as Sheldon whose turn-of-the century influence and later impact was significant makes him a worthy research topic. "Historiography affords a commentary on history that should inform any sophisticated probe into the subject," wrote Startt (1993, p. 24) in defense of doing history. Sloan (1993) agreed, and added that history provides a comparison that is helpful in assessing the past. Scholars study history to "understand the present through the knowledge of how the present came to be" (Sloan, 1993, p. 9) and to obtain help in understanding present problems with the idea of applying this insight "in facing the future," a partial quote from historian Frank Luther Mott, (Beasley and Ward, 1993, p. 12). Startt said historiography is "the craft of writing and interpreting history" (Startt, 1993, p. 17). This approach suggests the ideological view of Sloan (1991) and acknowledges the very personal matter of thinking about history based on each person's unique worldview.

The significance of Sheldon's work was his emphasis on his Christian faith coloring the newspaper content. This interplay of religion, particularly Protestant Christianity, must be a part of the research approach, according to Lukacs. Lukacs considered the study of religious history the most significant pursuit of historians because it addressed "questions of ultimate meaning" (Allitt, 1993, p. 15). Influenced by his Roman Catholic ideology, Lukacs recognized the dual nature of history for Christians who were confronted by the temporal and transcendental qualities of the events and ideas that most mark the important issues of life. Nonetheless, Lukacs determined that a true historical spirit could be attached to an interested love of truth in order to produce history that was creative and sanctified (p. 17).

For Sloan (1993), history can teach by providing a record of human experience (p. 8). Furthermore, history helps later generations understand more about the human condition, either individually or collectively. The idea is to grasp society and culture (Beasley and Ward, 1993; Carey, 1974) by examining the history of losers as well as winners, the ordinary person as well as the powerful. Considering the personal nature of historical research and the varying approaches, Gottschalk (1950) suggested that the writer reveal his or her assumptions.

The Use of Rhetoric to Understand The Jesus Experiment

This study of Sheldon, a clergyman-turned-editor, relies on a rhetorical approach as its method, which leans heavily on the cultural approach to historiography. The work focuses on Sheldon's practice of newswriting that he called Christian journalism, and is confined to a specific time and culture of American history.

According to the orthodox cultural interpretation, the media are not so much the result of deliberate efforts as they are the result of society acting on them (Startt and Sloan, 1989). A valuable tool for examining the way society acts on the media is the use of rhetorical analysis. Rhetoric "means the action humans perform when they use symbols for the purpose of communicating with one another" (Foss, 1996, p. 4). By examining the language that Sheldon used in his newspaper in general, and his editorials in particular, Sheldon's assumptions, both about publishing, and about the relationship between Christianity and journalism, can be better understood. Paired with his discussion of a Christian mainstream newspaper in a novel, *In His Steps,* rhetorical analysis helps make the manifest and latent goals of Sheldon's rhetoric more distinct. Rhetoric is used in many ways, including an attempt to share a personal perspective with an audience and to invite this person or group to "enter our world and to see it as we do, not in the hope that they will adopt our perspective but so they can understand us and our perspective better" (p. 5).

This kind of rhetorical criticism, a qualitative method, is used to look at the Jesus Experiment, the newspapers Sheldon published during the week of March 13, 1900, to March 17, 1900. This method helps the reader in understanding the artifact for what it suggests about the beliefs and values of Sheldon as a Christian who attempted to apply his faith to the craft of journalism. One of the many strengths of symbolic convergence theory is that it helps clarify values in a culture. Also known as fantasy theme analysis[4] (Griffin, 1997, p. 33), this method of rhetorical criticism examines "the shared worldview of groups of rhetors" (Foss, 1996, p. 121). University of Minnesota professor Ernest Bormann developed the theory of fantasy theme analysis to study communication in small groups (Griffin, 1997, p. 33), but this approach also is useful in examining the dramatic imagery and the group consciousness and solidarity of larger groups represented by subsets of the population that share ideology. "The theory explains the appearance of a group consciousness, with its implied shared emotions, motives, and meanings, not in terms of individual daydreams and scripts but rather in terms of socially shared narrations or fantasies" (Bormann, 1985, p. 128). Fantasy is the idea of "the creative and imaginative shared interpretation of events that fulfills a group's psychological or

---

[4] Fantasy should not be understood as a rejection of the divine truth of Holy Scripture. The term is used to capture the various facets of a narrative and its power to influence groups.

rhetorical need" (p. 130). Sheldon and his followers shared three fantasies.

1. They embraced the idea of all Christian believers that Christ was deity and each person must have a relationship with Him;
2. They embraced the idea that the mainstream general-circulation newspaper could be redeemed and be a tool to advance the first fantasy;
3. They embraced the theological assumptions of the Social Gospel movement, namely that they could advance Heaven on Earth through public policy reforms using the dominant communication tool of the day, the daily newspaper.

This research applies fantasy theme analysis (Bormann, 1972, 1973, 1976, 1982, 1983, 1985). This analysis is useful for "its ability to account for the development, evolution, and decay of dramas that catch up groups of people and change their behavior" (Bormann, 2000, p. 250). Based on symbolic convergence theory, the fantasy theme approach examines worldviews that are shared by people who embrace the view. These shared visions "structure our sense of reality in areas that we cannot experience directly but can only know by symbolic reproduction" (Littlejohn, 1996, p. 172). Groups fantasize during communication and this dynamic can lead to a chain reaction of fantasy where one or more participants in the group use symbols which may have unconscious meaning for others. Bormann's work examined the links between the symbols and imagery groups use and their group consciousness (Griffin, 1997, p. 32). This group consciousness can lead to a shared reality, which leads to a community of shared experiences and mutual understanding (Bormann, 1983, p. 104). The experience of the shared fantasy is the point and the group uses it to interpret other events. The fantasy theme provides the drama, the narrative, that is or becomes the reality for the participants. Fantasy themes are said to chain out when the fantasy becomes a rhetorical vision that provides a picture of reality for the group.

Bormann noted that fantasies often rely on fanciful scripts that are part of the narrative used in highlighting the group's hopes and fears. Bormann's theory is designed to account for the creation and use of special communication by examining communication in three steps.

1. The first step searches for repetitive communicative forms that suggest the presence of a shared group consciousness.
2. The second step seeks to describe what Bormann calls the dynamic tendencies within the communication system to help identify the effects group consciousness has in the formation of meanings, motives and communication within the group.

3. The last step examines the factors that support fantasies. The first two steps are descriptive, but the last, the most difficult, seeks to offer an explanation for the fantasy. Bormann noted that fantasies lead to predispositions for a predictable drama, a key feature in the bonding of participants into solidarity (p. 130).

Griffin noted that the use of symbolic convergence is useful to move from the small group context it originally described to a rhetorical vision that can be reinforced through mass media (1997, p. 34). For instance, consider farmers who fault the assistance of federal agents as unproductive in managing a cattle herd and their suspicion of a Washington, D.C., conspiracy. This shared vision can be ignited by phrases such as "Endangered Species Act" to suggest the collective hostility of farmers for lawmakers and the federal bureaucracy.

Rhetorical vision also explains when more than one fantasy theme drama combines to form a unified symbolic reality. Working from Bormann's theory, scholar Carl Wayne Hensley examined a religious movement to settle the American West that used as its motivation the parallel of winning the West to winning the world for Christ. According to Hensley, varied Protestant denominations rejected their previous differences to achieve the unity of the primitive church. The organizations had as their dramatic vision, the hastening of Christ's return. Known as the Disciples of Christ or just Christians, this group created a shared vision that called for adherents to become not only pioneers of the West but pioneers of reformation, and not only reject denominational creeds but also the old social order of the East. Hart (1990) noted that the Disciples of Christ fantasy themes demonstrated how people who take unpopular stands still flourish as a group through the solidarity of the fantasy theme (p. 334). The storyline sounded biblical: Disciples may be despised but their success is guaranteed.

Hart considered fantasy themes as mythic shorthands that help to punctuate a storyline with a clear past, present and future (p. 329). Unlike myths—which can be narratives that are transcultural—the fantasy themes are culture-specific. He noted that popular American idea that God chose the creation of the United States to deliver the world from its spiritual darkness could be considered a kind of myth.

The idea of religion and values can be used in another example of fantasy theme analysis when examining the public attraction to Ronald Reagan in 1984 over Jimmy Carter (Hart, 1990, p. 370). Reagan's characterization of America as promising and Carter's description of it as needy suggests a major theme in American Protestantism-Puritanism versus Evangelical Protestantism. The Puritan themes of predestination, wrath and punishment associated with Carter did not achieve the resonance of evangelical Protestantism of free will, mercy and forgiveness.

According to Foss (1996), symbolic convergence theory assumes that communication creates reality (p. 122). Hart (1990) found that all rhetoric is concerned about questioning popular assumptions by going beyond description of an artifact, or even interpretation, to evaluation of the possibilities suggested by the rhetoric and the conventional wisdom that ordinarily attends it (p. 24). Part of the power of rhetoric is the way symbols are used to make audiences comfortable (p. 25) or anxious. The reality creating function of symbols introduces order into the otherwise disturbing experiences of life (Foss, 1996, p. 122). While scholars debate the linkage between rhetoric and reality, critics tend to agree that the dynamic between symbols used in rhetoric and the reality audiences experience is valid.

Foss went on to argue that the symbol-reality couplet in symbolic convergence works for groups as well as individuals; hence, the idea of convergence. The shared experience of an audience centers on the shared fantasy, whereby it experiences the same emotions and moral values (Bormann, 1985, p. 131). "The result of sharing dramatizing messages is a group fantasy; the content of the dramatizing message that sparks the chain of reactions and feelings is called a fantasy theme" (Bormann, 1985, p. 131). The fantasy is said to chain out when one person allows his private symbolic world to overlap with another person's symbolic world to create a community of symbolic convergence (Foss, 1996, p. 122). The result is that the group experiences a similar response to the drama based on the fantasy theme, the imaginative interpretation (p. 123). The fantasy theme is a narrative the group shares that becomes the reality for those participants.

Like any drama, the fantasy has characters (Bormann, 1985, p. 130), a personae (p. 132), action, setting and characters (Foss, 1996, p. 123). For example, both Sheldon's novel and his newspapers use a cast of good characters and bad characters, heroes and villains, as well as action themes or plot lines. "The Experiment" section of this book examines this idea of a drama. The setting places the leading actors and the supporting actors in the scene while describing the scene, itself, with its own dramatic power.

Fantasy theme analysis, or symbolic convergence theory, allows the artifact to be studied by distancing this dramatic quality from the time it was presented. The audience engages the action not in the immediate context of the group but as part of a future conflict. Bormann said groups use fantasy like a script whereby the community can generalize from a specific incident, "thus, the archetypal fantasy has both the sense-making advantages of generalization and the persuasive power of the specific" (Bormann, 1985, p. 132). The use of scripts and the shared fantasy themes meld into a coherent rhetorical vision, then a rhetorical community (p. 133). With a vision that permeates a person's social reality, the symbolic system may be a "life style rhetorical vision; many of the religious and reform rhetorical visions in the United States fall into this category" (Bormann, 1985, p. 133). As an example, Bormann identifies a born-again Christian as the kind of person who adopts a lifestyle rhetorical vision and finds that the rhetoric changes his life.

The benefit of the shared fantasy is its ability to make otherwise confusing situations conform to an artistic and organized quality (Foss, 1996, p. 124), absorbing new and different experiences into a familiar pattern (p. 125). The themes are prejudiced to the shared ideas much as Carey (1989) suggested in his discussion of communication as ritualistic, saying it serves to help reinforce shared values and assumptions. Carey described two activities of communication, transmission and ritual. The dominant activity in communication is transmission—transmission of information, transmission of messages, particularly to encourage control by the sender over the receiver. Advertisers transmit information to persuade a consumer to purchase a product or service or to embrace an idea. However, communication may be ritualistic, a representation of shared beliefs that help maintain a society. Ritualistic communication serves a maintenance function in a society by reinforcing a sense of cohesion. Of the two roles of communication, Carey considered ritualistic communication to be superior because it helps explain the formation of reality for people. In mass media, the content of news need not vary drastically to fulfill the ritualistic function of information that is routine, familiar and comforting. The names and places in the news may change, but the basic conflicts reported do not and this dynamic provides an audience with a sense that all is well despite the tragedies and crimes. As in religion, the ritual has symbolic significance. The ritual also reflects the need for a community to be reminded of the shared ideas, beliefs and values in a society, as in the shared elements that are articulated in a weekly sermon from the clergy.

Fantasies can extend beyond ritualistic communication into argumentation by asserting assumptions that form the basis for the argument (Foss, 1996, p. 124). To be successful, an argument requires the acceptance of good reasons to engage a belief or action. Bormann's example of the Puritan vision demonstrates the privileging of revelation over empirical evidence. To engage this fantasy, participants assume that a deity revealed truth writ into a sacred text. The idea of divine truth notwithstanding, Bormann's point is that the assumptions undergirding the arguments reveal fantasy types that provide the ultimate legitimization for the beliefs.

Bormann's theory of symbolic convergence includes two assumptions. Assumption one is that communication creates reality for individuals and assumption two is that individual meaning for symbols creates a shared reality. In part, the use of symbolic convergence theory in this study demystifies the ideological framework undergirding Sheldon's work. The method for explicating an artifact is known as fantasy theme criticism or analysis, where the fantasy is the creative and imaginative interpretation of events. A fantasy theme is an abbreviated myth that pictures the values of a group and hints at some idealized vision of what reality can be. When a group participates in a shared fantasy, it achieves symbolic convergence where people are drawn together. A fantasy theme is the means through which the interpretation is accomplished in communication and often uses a word, phrase or statement to help the members of the rhetorical community to see the world in a certain way. The theme is a story that accounts for the group's experience and is the reality for the participants.

In his novel, as well as his newspaper, Sheldon's real world overlapped with the *In His Steps* fictional world of editor Ed Norman as a unique blend of fiction and reality. For Norman, his fictional city of Raymond was filled with a gradient of people who could be classed into two main groups. The first group was the people who did not attend church. They drank alcohol and this behavior led to lifestyle problems of family woe and unemployment; however, this group was powerless to remedy the situation and was confined to the kind of welfare cycle that critics accuse ineffective federal programs of promoting.

Most of the church members in Raymond, a fictional town that represents All-American towns, were people who were complacent about life and their faith as an energizing force for good. In this second group was a subgroup of committed believers who wanted to take action to make a difference in the lives of the community. They were the enlightened minority. Like the believing remnant suggested by Scripture, this group embraced the Gospel in a special way that was foreign to the other members of the church. The energized group was convinced that the world could be improved if individuals empowered with special insight would take action to redeem others. In this view of the world, the poor were incapable of helping themselves and were dependent on the energized church members for redemption. This vision of the world had no room for poor people who might rise to the challenge, exert strength to revolutionize their condition and produce a functional home life. The vision treated ordinary church members as those persons positioned on the precipice of enlightenment, yet short of making a genuine commitment.

From a fantasy theme perspective, each group exists with its own narrative. One group represents the tragic characters who play the roles of villains and victims of villains. The other group represents the hope of the community with the majority offering false hope or limited hope while the heroic minority represent the defenders who will vanquish evil and set the world right.

The saloon world described in *In His Steps* as the Rectangle was comprised only of people who were caught in sinful behavior. None of those who lived and drank there had any redeeming qualities. Unlike this dreary population, the private club of young gentry described in the novel had an appearance of respectability but its customers were not part of the believing remnant either. Sheldon mentioned their plight in his novel but dismissed their need in a few pages, choosing instead to focus on the more visible and more depressed condition of the inhabitants of the Rectangle. While the private club members and the Rectangle group, united by their use of alcohol, were in the same larger group of the unenlightened, the club members had the affluence to make a difference but not the motivation. The poor of the Rectangle had neither the will nor the means to make a difference in leading others to a life of reformation.

Fantasy theme analysis explores the meaning, emotion and motives for action as manifested in the message. Each of the groups described above declared their values by virtue of their chosen actions. In Sheldon's fictional world, the need to make a choice individually is a value to possess. The good choice always leads to good conduct, another value to possess. In Sheldon's newspaper, particularly his editorials, personal choice also is emphasized as a value to possess. It is highlighted repeatedly in his directive for abstinence, another value to possess. Abstaining from alcohol and abstaining from work on Sunday are important values in his world. Taken together with the other themes of Sheldon's fantasy, this approach suggests a world where rigid obedience to rules overshadows character. Rigidness dominates Sheldon's rhetorical vision where blind obedience outweighs the conversion of the heart.

Four Principles and the Rhetorical Vision

Four principles can be seen in this drama.

1. The world can be redeemed only through personal and individual reform;
2. Individual reform is the only path to lasting social reform;
3. Impoverished people are usually sinful and must depend on enlightened and often affluent people; in addition, the impoverished are powerless to participate in their own restoration (Ferre, 1988, pp. 15-42);
4. Those who neglect to ask "What would Jesus do?" still must participate in a divine contract that rewards good behavior and punishes bad behavior, on an individual as well as a group level. It is based on man's relationship to man and man's relationship to God, the basis of the Ten Commandments. This type of salvation is different from the classical position of evangelicals who insist that salvation is found in grace alone.

For Sheldon, the result of applying these principles would help usher in Heaven on Earth. His work could accelerate the Second Coming, which would end the kind of visible sin such as drinking that so distressed Sheldon. For Sheldon, this world would be a middle-class haven where people avoid sinful behavior such as drinking and smoking. In this New Jerusalem, the newspaper would gain the kind of prominence reserved for the Holy Bible and its pages would be used to inspire readers. For instance, on March 13, 1900, Sheldon featured a report of a great famine in India. "No paper in the United States had featured that item or given it any prominence," Sheldon wrote in his autobiography (1925, p. 125). "It seemed to me to be the most important piece of world news, and it went in on the front page of the first number of the paper, at the left-hand column which was the regular position the *Capital* had always given to feature news" (Sheldon, 1925, p. 125). In a break from newspaper convention of that day, Sheldon ran an appeal beside the news article and asked readers to send contributions to alleviate the suffering in India. The appeal provoked a fantasy chain reaction where the audience offered a common response to the imagery. Some readers literally gave money, but many agreed with the plan and endorsed the financial assistance even if they could not afford to make a donation themselves. By assenting, these readers briefly tasted the world that Sheldon envisioned where each person would help remedy a need according to his ability until the world would allow the lion to lay down with the lamb.

The response to the appeal can be considered part of the chaining of the fantasy. More than any other feature of the Sheldon edition, the response to the East Indian famine appeal prompted Sheldon to consider his newspaper a success. "Sometimes when people have asked me if the paper were not a failure, as the press reports for the most part said it was, I have replied that if it accomplished nothing more than saving several thousand children from starvation I would always feel as if the paper was a success, if it did nothing else" (Sheldon, 1925, p. 127). Publishing a news article side by side with an editorial was a convention Sheldon urged other daily newspapers to emulate. He said that the placement would ensure that readers would respond to the editorial comment. "If editorials are written to be read why not put them where the reader will read them?" Sheldon asked in his autobiography (1925, p. 126).

Mixing news and opinion is a tradition in the United States, and in early American journalism, news and opinion were combined. As early as 1721 an example of mixing news and opinion can be seen when James Franklin argued against smallpox inoculation in his *New England Courant* (Hollis, 1995, p. 76). By the Revolution, newspapers began isolating commentary and by 1840, Horace Greeley's *New York Tribune* had established a full page of editorial comment. By 1880, the editorial page, both prose and cartoons, was considered lively part of a newspaper and attracted readers (p. 77).

Naively, however, Sheldon assumed that by packaging news and commentary on the same topic on the same page, readers would have a uniform reaction to the information, and not challenge the message. Sheldon's rhetorical vision did not allow for complications or a gradient of responses. Like the behavior in his melodramatic novel, *In His Steps*, the behavior Sheldon advocated in his editorials was nearly self-evident. Once it was proposed, no questions seemed necessary. When Sheldon edited *The Topeka Daily Capital*, he drew on this worldview to advance this rhetorical vision that became a shared reality for his readers of the novel and his newspaper content.

In fantasy theme criticism, the basic unit of analysis is a word or phrase, and the question, "What would Jesus do?" works well as the phrase that engaged Sheldon's audience in seeing the world from an otherworldly vantage. For purposes of this book, this question will be known as the Jesus question. The worldview associated with the Jesus question is the center of Sheldon's rhetorical vision, which this study calls Spiritual Interrogation.

In symbolic convergence theory, the drama includes setting, characters and actions. In Sheldon's rhetorical vision, the setting was the newsroom in an urban location where hard-boiled men and women pursued information without regard for the individual consequence. In ordinary newsrooms, reform occurred when groups demanded action, usually by getting the legislature to pass a law. No attempt at individual reform was attempted. Only when groups reacted with a strong united front could social change occur. This group's rhetorical vision was materialistic; they considered legislation, not personal reform, as the mechanism to improve society. Personal choice was not the way to change the world; the world changed because powerful institutions demanded obedience.

In Sheldon's rhetorical vision, the press could be used to promote individual reform that would lead naturally to public policy reform. In his sermon on March 18, 1900, to his congregation at Central Congregational Church, Sheldon used a similar approach and compared nations to individuals ("Rev. Mr. Sheldon's Sermon," 1900). Because the newsroom world was hostile to Spiritual Interrogation, Sheldon's vision called for the posting of a code, like the Ten Commandments, that banned swearing, smoking or coarse behavior. As editor-publisher, Sheldon used the Jesus question to determine newsroom policy for others even if each staff member had not asked the Jesus question of himself or herself.

The setting for Sheldon's rhetorical vision included institutions outside the press that are marked by greed and selfishness, such as business and politics. Sheldon called for public-policy reform in these institutions in two of his six editorials. For Sheldon, all of life was fallen and only Spiritual Interrogation could lead to genuine reform. Like Augustine's *City of God*, Sheldon's world was the exclusive province of the spiritually enlightened, and anything outside that city was polluted. Business gouged customers, and politicians were bent by partisan considerations. The characters in this rhetorical vision were the same two groups found in the novel. The most wicked villains were the faceless purveyors of alcohol use. From the farmers who grew barley and hops to the manufacturers, distributors, vendors and customers of alcohol, this group was reserved for Sheldon's most caustic criticism. While some in this group possessed some affluence, they were not empowered with enlightenment from the Jesus question to offer any genuine assistance to others.

The characters who possessed power were Sheldon and all his readers who endorsed the idea of a Christian daily newspaper. His thinking said that a newspaper that "gives all the news, and in order to be conducted as a Christian newspaper should give news in such as way that it will entertain and instruct its readers without appealing to their baser passions, as so many of the newspapers of this age do" ("How the Saviour," 1900). However, Sheldon stopped short of a full treatment of his plan for the ideal newspaper, a Christian daily, and wrote, "I do not care to discuss the details of my plan, but rather wish to exert myself in making the newspaper what I believe it should be and letting it speak for itself" ("How the Saviour," 1900, p. 6).

According to Spiritual Interrogation, to possess spiritual insight, a character must ask the question, What would Jesus do?, then pray for an answer. The decision that seemed right, albeit unorthodox or uncomfortable, would be the right decision for that person. The lack of specifics characterized Sheldon's rhetorical vision. This subjective vision allows a range of responses as long as they were based on the Jesus question. The lack of specifics allowed readers to embrace ambiguity, knowing that no one can prove what Jesus' actions might be because Scripture portrayed the Savior as doing the unpredictable, including having a meal with sinners and publicans. This kind of behavior was seen as inappropriate in the First Century. The ambiguity of the Jesus question could be liberating for participants in the rhetorical vision who could explain a decision using the same vague reasons soprano Rachel Winslow used in talking to her friend Virginia Page in a scene from *In His Steps*.

"The fact is," Rachel was saying, after they had been talking a few moments, "I cannot reconcile it with my judgment of what Christ would do. I cannot tell another person what to do, but I feel that I ought not to accept this offer [to sing with the National Opera]" (Sheldon, 1994, p. 54).

In reviewing her management of her wealth, character Virginia Page remarked early in the novel that she was trying to discover a principle that would enable her to choose Christ's path (Sheldon, 1994, p. 47). Her friends told her it would take time but a sense of confidence would develop once she knew Christ better (p. 48).

Even this explanation remains vague, but it is part of the Spiritual Interrogation vision that put more authority on personal responses than a decision informed by a systematic study of problems using an approach based on reason. Inner peace was valued over outer, logical, even conventional responses.

When the fictional editor Ed Norman polled others who had asked the Jesus question whether they would publish a Sunday newspaper if it were in their power, Sheldon wrote in the novel *In His Steps*: "No one spoke for a minute. Then Jasper Chase said: 'We seem to think alike on that, but I have puzzled several times during the week to know just what He would do'" (Sheldon, 1994, p. 47). Again, the lack of standard answers to everyday questions gave the Jesus question its power to allow a person to be enlightened without prescribing any rigidity.

In Sheldon's rhetorical vision, the rank-and-file in the newsroom were participants in the experiment, but not the spiritually enlightened few. They obeyed orders. When reforming a person in poverty, the first principle was that a spiritually enlightened person must show the way to others who cannot help themselves. The enlightened person must be in a position of power and authority to have an impact.

Before and after the Sheldon experiment, J. K. Hudson was editor. He had editorial authority in *The Topeka Daily Capital* but not Sheldon's vision. He refused to participate in the Sheldon experiment (Ripley, 1965, p. 5). During the Sheldon experiment, Harold T. Chase was Sheldon's editor, a man Sheldon praised as "the one person who sat up nights with me and answered, or tried to, all sorts of questions about the technical details of the paper most of which displayed vast ignorance on my part, [sic] he wrestled with correspondents, and racked his brains to find fillers which would pass the censor [Sheldon], [sic] he must have felt many times like throwing the entire edition in the Hell Box [the trash], and he must have sighed the sigh of relief of his life when the ghost walked Saturday night [the newspaper was finished]" (Sheldon, 1925, p. 136).

On February 6, 1900, on page 6 of *The Topeka Daily Capital* (in the reprint of the full-page article from the *New York Journal* and Advertiser), Hudson wrote that he would not participate in the Sheldon edition. Hudson defended the press of his day, writing:

> The modern secular daily newspaper must be published everyday, give all the news of the entire world, and be made for all the people who read. This does not prevent the tone, politics and policy of the paper from being clean, honest and courageous in all questions affecting the rights and interests of the people, the state and the union. While the American daily press is no higher intellectually and morally than the people it is made for, it stands today as the most powerful protector of communities against crime, tyranny and corruption of officials, and as the greatest promoter of all public enterprises, and in my judgment making it conform to certain restrictions and limitations in order to bring it within the idea of a Christian daily would detract from, rather than add to, its influence and usefulness. (p. 6)

In Sheldon's rhetorical vision, the Hudson character had the strength and power to influence but was not part of the enlightened minority, so he could not help the disadvantaged or himself. The reporters and other staff members were not treated fully as individuals in Sheldon's rhetorical vision but acted as part of the background of stage props, necessary for color in the vision but without utility in advancing or foiling the goals to redeem the needy. Their function was as part of the machinery of the vision. Their job was to obey as part of a work ethic. The act of obedience, although celebrated in Spiritual Interrogation, did not empower them to be part of the enlightened minority unless they individually went through the steps of asking the Jesus question, praying, and making a personal decision.

The action in Sheldon's rhetorical vision was the appeal. Nearly every news article in the Sheldon edition and every editorial from March 13 to March 19, 1900, contained either a tacit or blatant appeal. The appeal did not ask the reader to ask himself, What would Jesus do? Instead, the appeal used a series of arguments from Sheldon's perch as the member of the enlightened minority to argue for actions that would contribute to the kind of world Sheldon considered possible if everyone was enlightened. Borrowing heavily from the Social Gospel and its emphasis on a personal response of good works following a spiritual experience, Sheldon considered Heaven on Earth to be possible. Without the scourge of alcohol, towns such as Raymond would be rid of most crime, family hardships and unemployment. These improvements alone would add to the New Jerusalem that the Puritans thought possible. Once the powerful business and legislative forces became enlightened, financial abuses would vanish and the public good would be genuinely served.

Buried deep within the appeal is Sheldon's fantasy theme–that genuine reform cannot exist without individuals performing Spiritual Interrogation, asking the Jesus question. Day after day, Sheldon's editorials urged readers to participate in good conduct and avoid bad behavior. He wrote of ideal person-to-person relationships and urged his readers to abstain from selfishness (March 13, 14 and 15) and to abstain from any connection to alcohol (March 14, 16 and 17). Sheldon also urged conduct for ideal person-to-God relationship, or proactive behavior. On March 13 and March 15, he told readers to obey God, that is, to seek the Kingdom of God; and in the March 17 evening newspaper, he told them to observe a day of rest. He implied as much in the March 13 issue.

In all these admonishments, Sheldon hinted at his rhetorical vision of the New Jerusalem that was possible if everyone was enlightened. In his last editorial, boxed on page one of the March 17, 1900 evening newspaper Sheldon wrote: "It is entirely possible for Christian civilization to be a great deal more powerful, useful, and intelligent, if everyone would take one whole day in seven to read what he does not read the other days of the week, to think what he does not think during the week, to rest, and pray, and commune with God as he does not during the week" ("The Saturday Evening Edition," 1900, p. 1).

To gain some background of this period and the press of the late nineteenth century, the next chapters explore the culture of the American society in 1900 to anchor this research in a cultural milieu. For purposes of these explorations, this research focus on the interrelationship of media with the environment, specifically the interplay of a clergyman-editor and his real-life display of ideas of Christian journalism. This work draws on Sheldon's blueprint for a Christian newspaper designed for a general audience that Sheldon first suggested in his fiction.

Summary

This chapter examined a variety of approaches to journalism history from the ideological, professional and cultural. This study is based on a cultural approach and examines the role of social forces in the development of Sheldon's experiment. In addition, symbolic convergence theory, a type of rhetorical analysis, is used in this study to examine the worldview of the groups of rhetors. Sheldon and his supporters shared an interpretation of events that relied on three fantasies, socially shared narrations.

1. They embraced the idea of all Christian believers that Christ was deity and each person must have a relationship with Him;
2. They embraced the idea that the mainstream, general-circulation newspaper could be redeemed and be a tool to advance the first fantasy;
3. They embraced the theological assumptions of the Social Gospel movement that assumed they could advance Heaven on Earth through public policy reforms using the dominant communication tool of the day, the daily newspaper.

In Sheldon's symbolic convergence , the shared vision was ignited by the phrase, "What would Jesus do?" to suggest the preferred position a person should assume on the issues of the day and a script to follow. The script supports a story that hints as an idealized vision of what reality can be. For Sheldon and his followers, the idealized vision was Heaven on Earth where everyone would practice temperance in a middle-class utopia. Sheldon's rhetorical vision depended on four principles.

1. The world can be redeemed only through personal and individual reform;

2. Individual reform is the only path to lasting social reform;
3. Impoverished people are usually sinful and must depend on enlightened and often affluent people, for the impoverished are powerless to participate in their own restoration (Ferre, 1988, pp. 15-42);
4. And those who neglect to ask "What would Jesus do?" must still participate in a divine contract that rewards good behavior and punishes bad behavior, on an individual as well as a group level. It is based on the Ten Commandments and a person's relationship to others and a person's relationship to God. For Sheldon, the result of applying these principles would help usher in Heaven on Earth.

Chapter 5

The Culture of Society of Sheldon's Day

The *fin de siecle* of the nineteenth century was captured in Jules-Alexander Grun's "Salon Des Artistes Francais," a painting that depicts an insouciant gathering of wealthy, well-dressed art patrons basking at an elaborate art exhibition (Daniel, 1987, p. 4). Beneath the pleasurable ambience suggested by that work of art, are the grave problems that presaged the coming twentieth century. The picture within the picture is of a world distracted by the glitter of new conveniences that promise a kind of freedom from the slavery of manual labor but hides the growing sense of detachment Americans and others endure. It previewed the years ahead when American children would toil up to 13 hours a day for pennies (Bohlander, 1992, p. 16), wealth would be concentrated among a minority and reformers would attempt to use politics, theology and sport to remake 1900 into Heaven on Earth.

Historian Howard Mumford Jones (1971) called the early part of the Gilded Age, 1865-1900, (Kobre, 1969, p. 305) the Industrial Age in America or the Age of Energy (1865-1883), while writer Daniel Boorstin (1973), former librarian of Congress, referred to it as the time of the Go-Getter, the person who takes advantage of opportunities. Both historians agreed that this period was a time of upheaval, revolution in the home, on the farm and in the city. Between the end of the Civil War, 1865, and the dawn of the twentieth century, the nation matured with expansion marking its industrialization, mechanization and urbanization (Emery et al 1996, p. 160). In the two decades before 1900 critics worried that unrestricted exercise of individual power by a minority of wealthy gentry could lead to both the misery of others and national weakness. This concern was just one of the themes that Sheldon highlighted in his Jesus newspapers.

Tragedy Times

The year of 1900 was full of tragedy, nationalism and a rush to consumerism. Despite an American team winning its first ever Davis Cup in competition on August 10, tragedy struck Americans at home and away. A hurricane and flood killed 8,000 on September 8 in Galveston, Texas (Bohlander, 1992, p. 8). Halfway around the world, China's Boxer Rebellion was underway. Begun on May 31, the Boxers threatened foreigners, and Christian missionaries in particular. The Boxers were a native patriotic society of discontented Chinese who trained in boxing and swordsmanship (Daniel, 1987, p. 14). American troops formed part of an expeditionary force to rescue whites, 300 of who were killed by the Boxers. Although the United States resisted the temptation to advance its colonial empire into China with the rescue, countries such as Great Britain continued a pattern of expansion. By 1901 Theodore Roosevelt supported an Open Door policy to increase America's influence but stopped short of seizing control in this part of Asia.

Progressive Spirit

The years preceding 1900 were marked by the Progressive spirit, which promised a better life with each passing year. Already a fever in the nation before the turn of the century, the Progressive optimism led to *The New York Times* citing 1899 as the year of unequaled prosperity. In a front page article on January 1, 1900, the Times borrowed a quote from banker James T. Woodward (Daniel, 1987, p. 10), boasting, "The United States [is] the envy of the world" (Bohlander, 1992, p. 11). Not to be outdone, the *Wall Street Journal* led its January 1, 1900, newspaper with an oxymoron, phrase that Wall Street was enduring prosperity panic. Even overseas, London reported that 1899 was a year of progress worldwide (Daniel, p. 10).

Expansionist Politics

The nation's growing sense of its own importance motivated international policy. On April 30, 1900, Hawaii became an official territory of the United States with President William McKinley pushing for this status because it was deemed crucial for the nation's international trade and military might (Daniel, 1987, p. 13). That same day in Vaughan, Mississippi, railroad engineer Casey Jones died trying to save passengers on a runaway train, making his name (not McKinley's) the subject of folk songs and myth. This combination of folk hero legend and American imperialism contributed to a national identity of a people who could do great acts because the Almighty had His hand on the land. This portrait may be the nation's most cherished–descendants of Puritans carving out a life in the new Promised Land and doing God's will (Hart, 1987, p. 233).

A year after Sheldon's famous Jesus newspaper ran in March 1900, the New York Public Library system was founded (Bohlander, 1992, p. 8), evidence to many of the civic improvements on the march. Yet, turmoil punctured hope when, on September 6, 1901, William McKinley, twenty-fifth president of the United States, was assassinated (Bohlander, p. 8)–but not before he had the United States adopt the controversial gold standard where $150 million gold reserve would be maintained to back legal tender. The controversy over gold or silver as a standard dominated the presidential election of 1896 (Mott, 1941, p. 577). Succeeding McKinley was Theodore Roosevelt, a loquacious New York City aristocrat, sworn in as president one-week later. Roosevelt was considered prime page-one material during this period, perhaps more than any previous president (Mott, 1941, p. 577). The brief Spanish-American War of 1898 had made a hero of Roosevelt and had won the Philippine islands from Spain. That war was considered the biggest story between 1892-1914 (Mott, p. 577). A naval base was built on the Philippines to protect America's international markets, leading critics to cry American imperialism. During the close of 1899, as the Twentieth Kansas Regiment (which fought in the Spanish-American War) presented itself at the Topeka State House grounds, Sheldon met at the home of F.O. Popenoe, owner of *The Topeka Daily Capital*, and they made their plans to publish the Jesus newspaper (Sheldon, 1925, p. 112).

Overseas, Britain continued its imperialistic conquests. From 1899 to 1902, the British fought the Dutch colonists, known as Boers, in Transversal and Orange, South Africa; in 1902 the Boers submitted to British rule.

During the war, Sheldon   received subscriptions to his Jesus newspaper, the number reaching 367,000 with one coming from Paul Kruger, head of the Boer republic (Sheldon, 1925, p. 115). Across the globe, nations such as Australia, India, Burma and Egypt extended their territories, with the British empire doubling in size before the end of the nineteenth century (Colton, 1968, p. 15). As U.S. president, Roosevelt championed another brand of Progressivism, improved quality of life through reform (Bohlander, 1992, p. 10), crucial because of the waves of immigration to America and within its regions.

Population Growth

Growth in population and industry climbed rapidly between 1870 and 1900 with 40 million people and 663 urban areas in 1870 reaching 75 million and 1,737 urban centers by 1900 (p. 10). In 1900 60% of Americans lived on farms near towns of less than 2,500 people, but by 1920, more than half the population lived in urban areas. Growth notwithstanding, this change worried Americans who thought life was becoming unnatural (Ferre, 1988, p. 3). Arthur M. Schlesinger, Sr. called the period between 1878 to 1898 "the rise of the city" (Emery et al, 1996, p. 157). More cities in the United States led to more public schools and greater literacy. The percentage of children in public schools rose from 57% to 72% with the number of high schools increasing from 100 in 1860 to 6,000 by 1900 (p. 159). In literature, two streams of readers developed as literacy improved and a mass market press developed. One group read the popular fiction of Arthur Conan Doyle and H. G. Wells while the other group focused more on classics (Magill, 1980, p. xiv).

The lure of the promised land in the United States attracted immigrants from overseas and factories lured southerners to the North and Midwest (Bohlander, 1992, p. 10). Immigration of mostly Roman Catholics and Jewish people swelled the nation from 75 million in 1889 to 100 million by 1917 (Ferre, 1988, p. 3). The nation's population, just 30 million at the close of the Civil War, was now a gathering of travelers, many poor and illiterate, who challenged the old order of rural values.

Corruption Found

Following the Civil War, corruption sank roots into cities. Perhaps the most egregious example was Boss Tweed who stole $200 million from New York City between 1868-1872, using an organization that began with a noble purpose, the Society of St. Tammany. The organization, founded in 1789, took its name from a Delaware Indian chief (Boorstin, 1973). The name Tammany came to mean friendship, and St. Tammany founder William Mooney created an organization that demanded loyalty in exchange for assistance with needs associated with city survival. Many of these Tammany members also joined the Democratic party and felt that public service meant help with finding employment, recovery from a fire, obtaining bail money–anything that was needed to live. The price was a vote, an unwavering vote for the candidates chosen by Tammany Hall.

Tammany Hall is a colorful example of the kind of corruption that occurred in a nation in transition, when its cities grew too fast for the utilities, where slums kept the middle class insisting on more police protection, and workers felt exploited by business. Despite bribes by Boss Tweed for newspapers' silence, in 1869 *The New York Times* and *Harper's* wrote about the misuse of public funds and scandals that plundered the city's treasury (Emery et al, 1996, p. 146). The scandal hurt New York politicians but tarnished national leaders, too, including President Ulysses S. Grant. It also illustrated the growing power of the press to influence reform. By 1904 this kind of reporting was becoming routine, with exposes such as Lincoln Steffens's *The Shame of the Cities*, an indictment against the rush from city to suburb using street car lines and the "scramble for franchises" to make a profit at the expense of orderly development (Boorstin, p. 105). The press at this period exhibited a "new indrawing power over the customers' minds and desires," and helped support a growing consumer culture of department stores and mail-order catalogues (Boorstin, 1973, p. 106). But aside from the commercial advantages, many thought that corruption, once exposed by the press, would lead righteous people to demand reform (Knowlton & Parsons, 1993, p, 179). "The spectacular plundering of a man like New York City's Boss Tweed, whose ring set a record for theft, were perhaps not so important as the setting of all politics into a mold of systematic corruption."

Greed was another problem, and regulation of big business motivated federal efforts in 1887 with the Interstate Commerce Act that required railroad rates to be reasonable and denounced monopolistic practices. In 1890 the Sherman Antitrust Act tried to block any restraint of interstate or foreign trade, yet both parties did not believe in regulation of big business. Laissez-faire, policies that said government could not regulate business, were changing (Ferre, 1988, p. 2), but the twentieth century would be well underway before the Sherman Antitrust Act could be amended to be effective.

Reform Spread

Corruption, coupled with urban growth and its city squalor and unbridled deceit in business and politics, ignited a series of programs for the needy (Bohlander, 1992, p. 14). In 1889, for instance, Jane Addams and Ellen Starr began Chicago's first settlement house called Hull House to aid the immigrants with food, medical care, employment, and child supervision for working mothers. Addams also supported the benefits of sports and believed in the idea that people from diverse cultures could gain social solidarity. She believed sports, whether enjoyed by a participant or spectator, could lead to reform in the city. A homogenous culture could be formed by uniting immigrants from different countries, particularly in the face of the tension of industrialization and urbanization of the late nineteenth century. "This industrialism has gathered together multitudes of eager young creatures from all quarters of the earth as a labor supply for the countless factories and workshops, upon which the present industrial city is based" (Addams, 1909, p. 5). Recreational parks, Addams contended, were the place where the blend of cultures could imbue the distinctively American citizen with a strong sense of fair play.

With the problems of rapid urban growth, governmental intervention became necessary despite the nation's tradition of political individualism (Magill, 1980, p. xiv). A belief in growing prosperity caused the poor to suspect the wealthy in the late nineteenth century, often called the "Gilded Age" (Bohlander, 1992, p. 12). Samuel Clemens, alias Mark Twain, coined the name Gilded Age to suggest the public's fascination with "millionaires, its goddesses and the millionaires' wives and mistresses." New York Central Railroad's Cornelius Vanderbilt, Standard Oil's John D. Rockefeller and Carnegie Steel's Andrew Carnegie captured the nation's imagination with their wealth (Bohlander, 1992, p. 12). For instance, Vanderbilt spent $3 million on his residence in Newport, Rhode Island, called The Breakers, site of some of the most extravagant parties of the day. But for an estimated 1.5 million children younger than 13 years of age who worked fulltime in the early 1900s (p. 16), labor was not training to become steel barons, but a means of survival. By 1938 Congress banned child labor. The untaxed fortunes of the Carnegies and others sometimes found their way into educational projects including small-town libraries and big-city projects including the University of Chicago, funded by J. D. Rockefeller.

Reformers looked to the state and federal legislatures to assist women who demanded full voting rights as part of the suffragists' movement (Bohlander, 1992, p. 17). In 1900 the suffragists' struggle was more than 50 years old, yet Wyoming, Colorado, Utah and Idaho were the only states that granted full voting rights, and these states possessed thin populations.

Agriculture Turmoil

In the Middle West, farm prices dropped on crops such as wheat, ruining farmers and leading to a profusion of sheriff sales in Kansas and Nebraska in the nineteenth century. The agrarian turmoil along with the depression of 1893 led to the political revolt known as Populism, that wanted to make government more responsive to farmers' needs (pp. 410-411). Mary Elizabeth Lease, a leader of the Populists movement in Kansas, urged farmers in speeches "to raise less corn and more hell." Others condemned foreign investment and Jewish bankers; Populists gained support across the country, forcing

Democrats in the West and South to either join or fight. It was this climate that drew William Jennings Bryan to champion the Populist vote with an anti-gold standard with his stirring line, "You shall not press down upon the brow of labor this crown of thorns, you shall not crucify mankind upon a cross of gold." This election pitted the agrarian vote against the industrialists and financiers (p. 414). Although Bryan lost to McKinley, the plight of farmers improved with price increases on farm produce just when crops failed abroad (p. 415). The Populist movement achieved its main objective of relief for farmers; moreover, it helped moved the economy from one based on individual control to one designed to protect the economically disadvantaged from the unimpeded exploitation of the wealthy and powerful.

It was during this period that Herbert Spencer and others insisted that the world was improving in a kind of natural process, and the new socioeconomic theory of individualism elevated the individual, as most important ingredient in the economic mix (Emery et al, 1996, p. 160). In this context, so the argument goes, the government should not interfere with the individual because he or she supplies the enterprise for progress, an application of Darwin's survival of the fittest idea, a phrase coined by Spencer.

Invention Solutions

Progress included the paper clip, patented in 1900, the photocopy machine, invented in France in 1900, Kodak's first Brownie cameras in 1900, and the hamburger, now an American icon, first served in New Haven, Connecticut, in 1900. It was around 1900 that baseball cards were first packaged with cigarettes and newspapers began adopting the four-column, tabloid-style. In 1900 the first wall-mounted telephone with separate ear piece and mouthpiece was introduced.

Charles Duryea founded the first U. S. automobile company in 1895, and by 1900 the Olds Company in Detroit opened the nation's first automobile factory, producing 400 automobiles during that first year. Nationally, fewer than 10,000 automobiles were produced worldwide in 1900, where one in 9,500 Americans owned an automobile; of that number, 40% of automobiles were steam-powered, 38% were electric, and 22% were gasoline-powered.

Religion Strong

By the turn of the century organized religion was under an open, intellectual assault. *The Quest of the Historical Jesus* by Albert Schweitzer focused on human relationships rather than systematic theology (Magill, 1980, p. xvi). Both Protestantism and Catholicism were confronting the social problems of urban expansion. From George Santayana to Friedrich Nietzsche and the Irish poet William

Butler Yeats, the intellectuals determined that society was decaying as values were challenged. As anarchy took hold, Christianity's comfort became less secure (Magill, p. xvii).

While theology was questioned, church membership lumbered side by side with population advances. In 1900 the surge of nineteenth century immigrants helped the United States Catholic Church expand to twelve million members. That same year Protestantism was established on every continent except Antarctica; in the United States, Protestants numbered six million Methodists, five million Baptists, 1.5 million Lutherans and 1.5 million Presbyterians.

Evangelists such as Dwight Lyman Moody inspired spiritual renewal among Protestants in the late nineteenth century (Noll, 1996, p. 288). Moody's timing was right and offered much comfort from the fears and concerns of failed Reconstruction in the South and the plight of cities. For Moody, reform must be from within and did not depend on society (p. 289). This message inspired other leaders, too. Throughout the 1880s Presbyterian A.T. Pierson organized conferences to attract 3,000 people for missionary service (p. 291). Even President McKinley, who exerted the nation's military might to gain control of the Philippines said his motivation came "as much from missionary as from national motives" (Noll, 1996, p. 292). He wanted "to educate the Filipinos, and uplift and civilize and Christianize them, and by God's grace do the very best we could by them, as our fellow-men for whom Christ died" (Noll, 1996, p. 293). In 1900 McKinley addressed the Ecumenical Missionary Conference in New York, where representatives of more than 200 missionary agencies heard ideas on spreading the Christian faith globally (p. 294).

Moody's idea of an individual's inward change that could lead to widespread societal change often manifested itself in campaigns against alcohol (p. 295). "Religious reaction to excessive drinking had begun in the early nineteenth century, at a time when Americans really were imbibing a great deal more than in previous generations" (Noll, 1996, p. 296). Prohibitionists fielded candidates in 1872 and 1892, but the platform was too narrow to succeed. Democratic populist William Jennings Bryan ran for president in 1896, 1900 and 1908 and "saw politics as a forum for promoting principles of a morality both Christian and American" (Noll, 1996, p. 300). Bryan's interest in rural America , when the nation was growing with cities and manufacturing, led to his demise politically, but he helped galvanize the thinking of many on issues such as the decline of the culture and evolution. He saw capitalists in the East as rapacious and bent on fleecing the innocent rural class (Ferre, 1988, p. 3). On evolution, Bryan urged farmers and workers to reject the imperialism of the elites, and their decadent moral system (Noll, 1996, p. 301).

Race Awareness

Along with the Progressive era of Bryan and Theodore Roosevelt, the South profited as well. Yet this liberal spirit did little to reach minorities. In 1883 the U.S. Supreme Court allowed private individuals or groups to continue discriminatory practices against Blacks despite laws that called for equal civil rights on state concerns (p. 618). In 1896 in Plessy versus Ferguson, a ruling about railroad train accommodations, separate but equal laws became the legal cornerstones for racial issues for the next 50 years. During this period, demagogues rose to power and called for white supremacy (p. 356). For the reformers, only economic progress could defeat old patterns of racial discrimination, but this solution led to pathological concentration of the dominance by a few industries such as oil, iron and steel, lumbering, and mining. By the turn of the century the notion of White and Black working together in the South seemed possible.

Social Gospel Influence

Overall, the ideas of personal action and public responsibility grew out of the Social Gospel movement, a theologically-based force from about 1880 to 1929, with the start of the Great Depression. At the heart of the movement was the idea that human institutions could substitute for the Kingdom of God (Beinart, 1999, p. 24). William Booth's Salvation Army, founded in the 1860s in East London, offered food, shelter, medical assistance, vocational training, education and other services to the poor and remains today the "most comprehensive Christian outreach to the cities" (Noll, 1996, p. 304). Its good works program expresses many of the tenets espoused in the Social Gospel with its emphasis on building Heaven on Earth.

Part of the Social Gospel's attraction was its reaction to the revivalists' emphasis on the individual at the expense of the realities of grim urban life (Ferre, 1988, p. 6). Among the iterations of the Social Gospel was a conservation kind where personal moral enlightenment would lead naturally to societal improvement. Conservative clergy such as Joseph Cook and Minot J. Savage saw a connection in fewer labor clashes with a voluntary increase in a worker's pay. A more strident Social Gospel approach leaned on socialistic policies for improved life. Christian socialists including W. D. P. Bliss and George D. Herron urged a rejection of democratic capitalism for a brand of socialism that would lead to a Christianized social order. Centrists included theologians such as Washington Gladden, Richard T. Ely and Walter Rauschenbusch, "who emphasized the immanence of God in human affairs, the relevance of Christian love to the economy, and the increase of beneficence in social relations" (Ferre, 1988, pp. 6-7). As Sheldon would do in his Jesus newspaper, Raushenbusch condemned business as unregenerate with its wealth relegated to a minority (p. 8).

Behind the Social Gospel movement were a number of theologians from the nineteenth century who wanted to interject feeling into faith (Grenz & Olson, 1992, p. 39). Friedrich Schleiermacher, the father of modern theology, initiated liberal Christian theology (p. 40). He argued that what can be known does not have to be limited to sense experience, a restriction established by a number of philosophers, particularly Immanuel Kant (p. 43). Before Schleiermacher, the rule of natural law discounted the idea of miracles and the supernatural, but Schleiermacher's theology was based on human experience, intuition. For Schleiermacher, the bridge that connected the otherwise impassable gulf between rationalism and orthodoxy was a feeling, the feeling of utter dependence on God (p. 44).

Schleiermacher influenced the development of liberal theology's emphasis on "the freedom of the individual Christian thinker to criticize and reconstruct traditional beliefs," and focused on the "practical or ethical dimension of Christianity" (p. 52). These and other features encouraged liberal theologians to emphasize "the kingdom of God as a historical, ethical society of love . . ." (Grenz & Olson, 1992, p. 52). According to Grenz and Olson, the leading liberal theologian in the late nineteenth century was Albrecht Ritschl, who offered Christianity an out from the onslaught of science that seemed to rob the faith of confidence in its ability to know religious knowledge (p. 53). Ritschl's religious knowledge was concerned with "the way things ought to be" (Grenz & Olson, 1992, p. 54). Ritschl succeeded in gaining support for God's redemption of humanity in the kingdom of God and encouraged the direction of the Social Gospel for good works (p. 58).

Following Ritschl was the German scholar Adolf Harnack who focused on the kingdom of God as the ideal for humanity (p. 60) and Walter Rauschenbusch, who lived in Hell's Kitchen, a needy area of New York City. Rauschenbusch criticized the wealth gap in America "and asserted that being a Christian in this social crisis meant working for the salvation of economic structures that perpetuate poverty" (Grenz & Olson, 1992, p. 61). As Sheldon would do in his Jesus newspapers, Rauschenbusch condemned runaway capitalism and called for corporate entities to repent and be saved. Rauschenbusch used an evangelical fervor to urge a restructuring of major industries and the dismantling of an economic system base on greed and profits, measures that he and other advocates of the Social Gospel thought could bring the kingdom of God on earth.

Intellectual Issues

Behind the jarring changes in theology in the nineteenth century were the philosophical movements that undermined ideas of truth and objectivity while scientific advances demonstrated awareness of an unseen world of germs and a need for sanitation (Magill, 1980, p. xiii). In 1900 German philosopher Nietzsche died, but his *Thus Spake Zarusthustra* on the death of God and the power to will stirred thinkers on several continents. In 1900, Max Planck proposes quantum theory and Sigmund Freud published *Interpretation of Dreams* (Puente, 1999, p. D2). Tocqueville remarked early in the nineteenth century that he doubted that the United States could ever make an intellectual contribution. But the Michelson-Morley experiment of 1887 established that the idea of ether as a standard of absolute space did not exist, and prepared the way for Albert Einstein. By 1905 Einstein set forth a special theory of relativity that ultimately led to a revision of Newtonian physics and his famous equation–E=mc squared–that described the reciprocal qualities of energy and mass (Magill, 1980, pp. xv-xvi).

While Sheldon would address spiritual issues in his Jesus newspaper, disasters and wars in the proceeding years laid a foundation for his coverage and commentary. In 1897, an earthquake, the most powerful one ever recorded, struck Assam, India, but few deaths were reported. In 1899, millions died of starvation in India (Daniel, 1987, p. 10), an issue that Sheldon used to mobilize the American nation in his Jesus newspaper. Sheldon highlighted suffering from natural calamities, but spoke against suffering in sports such as boxing; in 1905 the nation took that idea to heart with a public outcry against the increasing roughness of football games following a season in which 18 deaths and 159 injuries were reported in college football.

Heightened awareness marked the late nineteenth century. The Civil War created an awareness of ready-to-wear clothing, which contributed to a wave of standardization (Boorstin, 1973). Following the Spanish-American War, the United States was plunged into world politics and it needed standards for its products. With this standardization of material came the rise of experts in medicine, engineering and statistics (McCormick, 1990). Alongside this new class of considerable influence arose the consumer class that could be seduced by bright lights and an invitation to imagine ownership.

Consumer Culture

In Paris, the unofficial capital of Europe, the Paris Exhibition of 1900 led to a revolution in consumer behavior (Williams, 1996, pp. 187-193). Covering 547 acres, the exposition opened April 14, 1900 (Daniel, 1987, p. 13) and attracted 50 million people worldwide (Williams, 1996, p. 187). Exhibitions began in London in 1851 and continued during 1855, 1867, 1878 and 1889 until the climax at the 1900 Paris exhibition. All but the Paris exhibition had the same theme: to teach "a lesson of things" (Williams, 1996, p. 187). While early expositions such as the 1878 exhibition concentrated on the scientific discoveries of electricity and photography, the Paris Exhibition was bent on entertaining visitors from around the world. Earlier exhibits displayed the history of labor and tools from all eras but the 1900 exposition celebrated consumption over "abstract intellectual enjoyment the progress of knowledge" (Williams, 1996, p. 188).

The sensual pleasures of the exposition demonstrated the consumer revolution that was coming. Williams (1995, p .189) wrote:

> From earliest history we find indications that the human mind has transcended concerns of physical survival to imagine a finer, richer, more satisfying life . . . But in the late nineteenth century, commodities that provided an approximation of these age-old longings began to be widely available. Consumer goods, rather than other facets of culture, became focal points for desire.

The 1900 exposition, seen as prophetic, broke with the past and suggested the consumer revolution that was coming (p. 189), if not in the United States, at least in France. Merchandising, a common marketing practice today, characterized the 1900 exhibition where exhibitors appealed "to the fantasies of the consumer" (Williams, 1996, p. 189). The confirmation of this development was the opening of department stores, where items receive a fixed price (no haggling), and consumers could look without an expectation to buy. "In exchange for the freedom to browse, meaning the liberty to indulge in dreams without being obligated to buy in fact, the buyer gave up the freedom to participate actively in establishing prices and instead had to accept the price set by the seller" (Williams, 1996, p. 190).

In addition to inflaming a customer's imagination to desire a purchase, the exhibition created a fantasy land hitherto only available in his imagination. Electrical power to light up incandescent and arc lights was used to create a make-believe world of "falling rainbows, cascading jewels, and flaming liquids" (Williams, 1996, p. 191). Soon advertisers to spotlight new fashions in department store windows or promote a trade name, all in the name of consumption (p. 192) commandeered these lights.

Summary

The world that Charles Sheldon confronted when he took charge of *The Topeka Daily Capital* for one week was one characterized by turmoil. Intellectuals of the day evaluated the decaying mores and determined that the West was in trouble. Leaders such as Bryan urged reform to combat the oppression of farmers; others such as Moody campaigned for inner renewal as the cure. Sheldon joined the reform movement to denounce the concentration of wealth and the corruption caricatured in the figure of Boss Tweed. With his Jesus newspaper, Sheldon hoped to demonstrate how the press could use its daily contribution to show individuals the path to reform. His newspaper with its evangelical pleas was designed to call for reform without resorting to the sensationalism evidenced in the coverage of the Spanish-American War of 1898. Politics, greed, and undisciplined behavior attracted Sheldon's attention, along with his conviction that once individuals changed inwardly, true reformation could characterize a society reeling and jarred from the turmoil of change. To understand the press of this era and the ways it compared to and contrasted with Sheldon's newspaper, the next chapter focuses on the culture of the press of the late nineteenth century.

Chapter 6

What Were Newspapers Like in Sheldon's Day?

A Challenge to Sensationalism

Sheldon's experiment, while novel for its blatant advocacy of Christianity, was not so different from the American press of the period or from earlier periods. In the 1940s, the *North American* in Philadelphia produced a newspaper free of suggestive advertising and teeming with morality (Miller, 1987, p. 104) It failed. Two decades later in June 1960 the *New York Sun* tried its approach to publishing front-page articles on church events and by August the was revamped into a religious paper that banned ads for vices such as liquor and theater (Miller, 1987, p. 104). It returned to a secular content by late 1861. Yet another failed attempt was tried and abandoned by the *Boston Daily News* in 1869 following the scandal of a minister closely associated who fled the country in the wake of revelation that he had committed forgery (Miller, 1987, p. 104.)

By 1883 and 1900 American journalism was characterized by invention, innovation and ingenuity, leading historians to call it the Age of New Journalism. Publishers such as Joseph Pulitzer and William Randolph Hearst made headlines in the late nineteenth century and continue to dominate press history today. When Charles Sheldon launched his Jesus newspaper in 1900, his experiment sought to challenge the sensational style, in much the same way Adolph Ochs did when he set a new course for the urban *The New York Times* in 1896 (Stephens, 1997, p. 239). Ochs made his reputation in New York while editors such as William Allen White's *Emporium Gazette* gave the

Midwest a stentorian voice with conservative editorials such as "What's the Matter with Kansas?" That famous article that defended business development and found a secondary audience when the piece was reprinted by most of the country's Republican newspapers (Stephens, 1997, p. 259). By the time of Pulitzer and Hearst, the press was thriving business, having survived a Civil War, partisan politics and rapid mechanization with its demands for standardization and rigid deadlines (Folkerts & Teeter, 1989, p. 255). An inexpensive papermaking process and rapid printing helped the press serve a burgeoning urban population that depended on accessible information (p. 256).

A Challenge to the Status Quo

Sheldon's newspaper also borrowed from the traditions of the colonial press where political authorities were questioned. Early press history often is written from the Progressive school that focuses liberty overcoming repressed rights. Seventeenth century philosopher John Locke detected this observation and argued that inalienable rights are ordained by God and include the notion that man is free and all men are equal (Altschull, 1990, pp. 49-54).[5] Locke also said that men institute government and this institution derives its just powers from the consent of the governed (Knowlton and Parsons, 1993, p. 33). One press account put the idea this way: "Part of the story has as its theme the continuing efforts by men and women to break down the barriers that have been erected to prevent the flow of information and ideas, upon which public opinion is so largely dependent" (Emery et al, 1996, p. vii). The barriers can refer to press restrictions such as the British Stamp Act of 1765, a tax on newspapers, and the Alien and Sedition Acts of 1798, a law passed by Americans to control opinionated editors and publishers. The barriers also may refer to the organic issues of life in the colonies, "the physical basis" (Lee, 1937, p. 20). These challenges could include obtaining paper, presses, and the other material needed to publish in the late 1700s. However, the barriers can take on a philosophical theme, akin to the idea that the Puritans had about a divine mandate to possess New England (Cressy, 1987, p. 75). In summary, many press accounts of this period suggest that America was destined to succeed through its savior, the indomitable press, and the cleansing power of democracy.

---

[5] These philosophers wrote about men with the understanding that the principles apply to both men and women; however, Locke among others betrays inconsistencies in his ideas as they apply to non-whites.

A Challenge to Sports Coverage

Sheldon also thought that his newspaper could overcome obstacles such as the inclusion of content Sheldon considered inappropriate for family readers. For instance, he opposed news of violent sports such as boxing. Sheldon saw his newspaper as a tool of reform, but in designing his Christian daily, he wrote that crime, scandal, and sensational divorce cases were missing in his newspapers because "it is a childish and useless way to depict human frailty simply for the sake of creating a mental sensation in the reader" (Sheldon, 1925, p. 131). Sheldon said he modeled his newspaper after the Bible, where crime is "reported briefly and the emphasis placed on the cause, and the remedy, which is the only scientific way to report crime" (Sheldon, 1925, p. 131). Sheldon's allusion to science was part of the age's fascination with the empirical method; however, Sheldon's rhetorical vision was based on revealed truth, not scientific truth. He tried to buoy his argument for no sensational news by arguing that the world was evolving for the good and that he was a pioneer in an enlightened journalism that would eventually become the standard. Sheldon wrote, "The rule that was observed during the week was the rule of the Bible method, and in time that rule will be observed by all the daily press" (1925, p. 131).

A Challenge of Political Dependence

Early American newspapers typically consisted of four pages, about the size of ordinary typing paper, and were dominated by religious essays along with short news items (Sloan, 1991b). Sheldon saw his newspaper as part of this tradition, with eight broadside pages, but with the added benefit that no political authority could censor him for unpopular content, as was the case of Benjamin Harris. Harris is credited with publishing the first American newspaper, *Publick Occurrences*, on September 25, 1690. It lasted one issue and offended the Puritan clergy and royal governor (Kobre, 1969, p. 3). The episode concerns a printer who suffered for telling the truth; yet Harris made a career of illegal journalism in the name of truth telling (Clark, 1991, p. 250). From 1673 until 1679 in London, Harris "published a number of religious books, several of which attacked Quakers and Catholics," and served time in an English prison for his criticism of King Charles II (Sloan, 1996, p. 49).

By 1723, another Boston printer managed to challenge the political forces and survived by offering an alternative publication, a practice Sheldon employed in his experiment. The *New-England Courant* is steeped in controversy from its inception over its contribution to the development of a free press. Benjamin Franklin's half-brother James began the *New England Courant* in 1721 at the suggestion of others to amuse themselves with their own prose and to challenge the Puritan-dominated *Boston Gazette*, a paper James Franklin once printed (Kobre, 1969, p. 21). To be more precise, the *Courant* began as a protest "not to free Bostonians from religious control, but as part of a long-term effort to destroy Puritan popularity and establish in its stead the Church of England as the official church in Massachusetts Bay and the other colonies in North America" (Sloan, 1991a, p. 109).

James Franklin's *Courant* challenged the religious and political order and "helped establish the tradition of editorial independence" (Emery et al, 1996, p. 27). By 1722, however, James Franklin was charged with contempt for writing that the government did not have an effective defense against pirates in the area. Franklin served prison time but refused to recant, provoking the religious and political authorities to forbid him from printing the *New England Courant* (p. 28). In 1723, James Franklin circumvented the colonial order not to publish by making his half-brother Benjamin, a printer apprentice, the *Courant*'s publisher. Benjamin Franklin used the transition to abandon his apprenticeship and start printing legally in Philadelphia.

Despite the evasion of the law, James Franklin's example showed "that when a newspaper is aggressive and readable in serving the public cause, it will elicit support sufficient to protect it from powerful foes" (Emery et al, 1996, p. 28). Press rights notwithstanding, the *Courant* also served a "truly literary purpose" (Clark, 1991, p. 261) and its work set "the stage for two other literary newspapers, the *News England Weekly Journal* and the *Weekly Rehearsal*, both the playthings of clever young dilettantes" (p. 262). The *Courant* used sarcasm to ridicule rivals, carried crusades on smallpox inoculation, and encouraged discussion of issue in essays. At its worst, it launched bitter attacks on Puritan clergy including Increase Mather and his son Cotton Mather over an inoculation against smallpox (Kobre, 1969, p. 24). Franklin argued against the inoculation.

A Supporter of Religious Zeal

Lost in this narrative, however, is the commitment to a religious ideal, the characteristic of interest to Sheldon as he developed his Christian newspaper. Sheldon thought that a Christian daily newspaper could advance the Kingdom of God ("New opportunities," 1899, pp. 24-26). While the *Courant* attempted to challenge the dominant religious order of its day, Sheldon's newspaper attempted to challenge the powerful forces of his day, particularly the spirit's industry.

Sheldon used Christianity as the source for his views on issues. This idea is not without precedent. As a vocal supporter of Anglicanism,

Checkley openly preached that his faith was the only true religion, that
the Church of England was the established church in America and the
Puritan clergy were illegitimate. The *Courant* was his forum and he
supported it. Sloan characterized the *Courant* as unpopular and
unrespected, noting " . . . the *Courant*, as the historian Edward Wilson
previously has shown, did not provide a landmark in the history of
freedom of the press; it simply continued a practice of outspoken
opinion already begun by Boston's other newspapers and pamphlet
writers" (1991a, p. 141). As an influence, the *Courant* is important for
its commitment to publishing opinion and its support for independent
religious thinking (Kobre, 1969, p. 26), two issues that characterized
Sheldon's Jesus newspaper.

Both the Harris case and the Franklin episode are used to argue that,
with time, the American press became bolder and more assertive of its
freedom of press rights, a Progressive interpretation of history. The
cases also are used to demonstrate the gradual and steady improvement
of the press as it developed into the modern version where reporters
seek information, interview sources, and investigate records to satisfy
the public's right to know. A more basic function is at work, however.
The goal of a newspaper is to retain an audience by contributing to the
folkways, common modes of behavior, and mores–correct ways of
thinking and behaving (Lee, 1937, p. 37). The content serves to provide
guidance to readers on life, an issue Sheldon addressed in his Jesus
newspapers. Sheldon said the press could be a key factor in the eternal
salvation of a community ("New opportunities," 1899, pp. 24-26).

Historians sometimes focus on the ideological conflict where news
gatherers rallied on the side of liberty and democracy against "the
powerful forces of wealth and class" in a fight for economic rights for
all (Startt and Sloan, 1989, p. 29). Sheldon followed this model as well.
For instance, on Thursday, March 15, 1900, the front page carried a
three-column illustration depicting a man lying about his taxes. Near
the illustration was an article on tax dodgers. Sheldon began and ended
the article written by George B. Harrison with notes from the editor.
The first note said church members and respectable people lie about
their taxes. "Apply the moral for yourselves," he wrote (Sheldon,
1900k, p. 1). At the end of the article, Sheldon wrote:

> Is it any wonder in view of these facts that bitterness
> is felt by the poor for the rich? Is it a wonder that
> there is not more of it? The chasm that yawns
> between the working man and the man of wealth will

never be filled up as long as the above facts remain to disgrace our Christian civilization (p. 1).

On a more pragmatic basis, the role of newspapers is to satisfy the ancient need to be informed and participate in a community (Lee, 1937). In the late 1700s coffee house owners kept newsbooks, which helps explain the reason daily newspapers were not needed until the early 1800s. When ships docked, any news the captain possessed was written in a book for the clientele to peruse. Readers could learn the news and share socially in these establishments. The activity fulfilled the transmission and ritual communication needs for readers who benefited as much from the act of reading information of interest to a community as they did in the knowledge it afforded (Carey, 1989). For example, Samuel Gilbert's Exchange Coffee-House provided news in newsbooks in the late 1700s. Gilbert revolutionized the practice in 1811 when he hired the enterprising Samuel Topliff, Jr., to meet incoming ships to obtain news from arriving ships all the faster (Kobre, 1969, p. 163). This innovation led to the formation of the first press association in the 1840s, which meant more news, more variety of news and less delay between the gathering of news and its dissemination; yet the purpose of the news remained the same. News linked a community by highlighting information that news gatherers and news readers agreed formed the basis on a shared view of reality. With each advance in the collection and dissemination of news, participants from all sides debated the content, denouncing some as reckless or unworthy of press and, sometimes, offering a suggestion on alternatives that were more in keeping with their particular worldview, a notion Sheldon embraced when he edited the Jesus newspaper in 1900.

Sheldon's experiment is most often faulted for its spotty news coverage. The rival evening newspaper in Topeka, the *Topeka State Journal*, enjoyed a circulation surge the week of Sheldon's experiment. Its circulation increased 40% because of "the paucity of both local and national news carried in Mr. Sheldon's *Capital* (Ripley, 1965, p. 28). In addition, the *Topeka State Journal* demonstrated its news gathering acumen by trying to beat any news that Sheldon's newspaper could break. For instance, Sheldon reported generally about corruption in the inequitable personal property taxes while the *Topeka State Journal* provided a specific list of personal property assessments of 259 firms and individuals whose assessments were in excess of $1,000 ("Greater Topeka," 1900, p. 1).

A Challenge to the Journalism of Hearst and Pulitzer

This brief review of highlights from the American press and the ideological tension represented by it forms the basis for a foundation on which to examine the late nineteenth century and the themes that influenced press criticism in the time preceding Sheldon's experiment. As the population grew in the nineteenth century, so did the number of daily newspapers with the largest increase between 1880 and 1890, an increase of 686 daily newspapers resulted in a total of more than 1,500 (Everett, 1996, p. 276). The increase was due to the flight to the city by rural Americans and the swell of immigrants to urban areas in the 1890s (p. 275). By 1890, a third of the United States population lived in the city. Increased literacy and increased travel from improved transportation contributed to a high saturation of newspaper circulation with one paid newspaper subscription for every two people in the United States. The abundance of inexpensive newspapers with an ample supply of opinion content, while praised for the quantity, was condemned for telling readers what to think. Rather than contributing to the mores of a community, the newspaper was imposing views.

Imposing views was the hallmark of two publishers from this era, an immigrant and a wealthy imitator, William Randolph Hearst and Joseph Pulitzer. The immigrant who spoke English as a second language was Joseph Pulitzer, a Hungarian who knew readers would respond to crime and sports and who packaged his content to be bigger than life– "cheap but bright, not only bright but large, not only large but truly democratic" (Boorstin, 1973, p. 403). Pulitzer's *World* sold for two cents a copy and became the nation's first modern mass-circulation daily with circulation of 1.5 million. Although the Penny Press began with Benjamin Day of the *New York Sun* in 1833, Pulitzer and others continued the tradition of inexpensive newspapers available without a subscription.

Pulitzer arrived in America in 1864 and joined the Union Army. The Austrian army rejected him because of his weak eyes and frail physique but the Union Army took him gladly, after three years of battle had made it desperate for soldiers (Olasky, 1991, p. 109). Pulitzer cleaned up after the Union mules and fared poorly as a soldier (Kobre, 1969, p. 374). "From this experience he developed a lasting antipathy toward militarism" (Kobre, 1969, p. 375). During the war, Pulitzer worked with Carl Schurz, a cavalry regiment commander. Later Schurz established a German-language newspaper in St. Louis and hired Pulitzer in 1868 (Everett, 1996, p. 286). Despite his poor English, Pulitzer excelled, working hard, sometimes from 10 a.m. to 2 a.m. daily, first at a German-language newspaper and in 1878, at his own

English-language newspaper (Kobre, 1969, pp. 374-375). Soon Pulitzer expanded and created the *St. Louis Post-Dispatch*, a newspaper that proved so profitable that Pulitzer could finance the purchase of the *New York World* in 1883.

With the *World*, Pulitzer drew on his own experience to target this growing immigrant audience with "easy-to-read, gripping stories (good for learning English) with economic envy" (Olasky, 1991, p. 110). While immigrants relied on newspapers for cues on proper behavior in the city (Schudson, 1978, p. 98), "city newspapers had become street cars of the mind" (Boorstin, 1973, p. 106). Before long, the *World* crusaded to eliminate the evils of monopolies, and championed the rights of unions, supported an eight-hour work day, worked for the abolition of bridge tolls and promoted the funding of a $100,000 pedestal to support the Statue of Liberty (Kobre, 1969, p. 382).

Despite Pulitzer's commercial success, some regard him as a scoundrel who savored vilifying clergy. Pulitzer used journalism as a weapon to avenge himself on his oppressors, particularly those who took advantage of his poor knowledge of English during the Civil War to make him the butt of practical jokes. With his *St. Louis Post-Dispatch*, Pulitzer found a market for gossip and salacious stories and focused on the clergy as a target for his exaggerated news coverage (Olasky, 1991. pp. 109-110). Once Pulitzer reported a clergyman as drunk and insulting to a woman on a streetcar. The minister inadvertently breathed into the woman's face and she smelled alcohol; that was later revealed to be a medicine with an alcohol base. Pulitzer liked the combination of sex-and-sin content in his pages, and the formula worked to increase circulation, particularly among the growing population of immigrants (Emery et al, 1996, p. 177). Pulitzer also was known for the human-interest story and stunts such as reporter Nellie Bly's globe-trotting around the world in less than 80 days.

Olasky (1991) considers Pulitzer an imitator of the Puritan press by his emphasizing bad news to draw attention to the need for change (p. 111). However, the Puritans wanted to expose humankind's corruption to lead to God's grace, whereas Pulitzer wanted to build an empire that was above the power of the presidency. Pulitzer said that the president came from partisan politics and was elected to a four-year term, but the *New York World* is not bound by terms and is free to tell the truth (Olasky, 1991, p. 111). By now, the issue facing the free press was not ideological conflict but the danger that absolute press freedom could lead to irresponsible journalism. The Consensus school championed publishers such as Adolph Ochs, who, in the 1800s, shunned Pulitzer's sensational techniques to emphasize news over opinion (Startt and

Sloan, 1989, pp. 34-35). The Consensus school argued that agreement, not conflict, marked history; belief in democracy and freedom helped the press work with institutions such as government to improve life.

While Ochs was the contrast to Pulitzer, William Randolph Hearst was his shadow (Everett, 1996, p. 286). Hearst, who challenged Pulitzer, continuing in what has become known as the sensational style of journalism long after the others of the era stopped (Emery et al, 1996, p. 194). Hearst is as much an enigma as Pulitzer. From an affluent background, he went to Harvard, drank too much, and idled away his time listening to music. He was suspended for celebrating Grover Cleveland's election to the presidency with a fireworks display and was later expelled for decorating chamber pots with the likeness of the faculty, including the legendary William James (p. 196). While on the East Coast, Hearst became interested in Pulitzer's *World* and the stage was set for Hearst's challenge to New York publishing a few years later.

William Randolph Hearst was the son of George Hearst who had made his fortune in mining. George Hearst bought the *San Francisco Examiner* in 1880 and served as a U.S. senator. The elder Hearst gave the younger Hearst the *Examiner* in 1880. By the time William Randolph Hearst died in 1951, he had built a media empire. "At one time Hearst also controlled the International News Service, three radio stations, and four or five magazines, went to Congress, was enthusiastic for Franklin D. Roosevelt and then bitterly opposed him" (Jones, 1971, p. 117).

The empire began with the *San Francisco Examiner*, in which Hearst imitated Pulitzer in the use of pictures, crusades and content designed to entertain readers (Riley, 1996, p. 289). In 1890, Hearst purchased the *New York Journal*, hired away Pulitzer's best staffers and mounted a successful challenge to Pulitzer's growing circulation.

The period, known as the age of New Journalism, was marked by increased wealth and a growing middle class who found light content, crime reporting, and non-news content attractive (p. 280). For Hearst and Pulitzer, New Journalism expanded to its logical but exaggerated end, concluding in "yellow journalism." Yellow journalism emphasized large type headlines designed to shock and scare readers. It received its name from Richard Outcalt, creator of the Yellow Kid comic strip. When Hearst raided the *World*, he hired Outcalt, then a popular cartoonist (Folkerts and Teeter, 1989, p. 271). As Hearst and Pulitzer intensified their circulation wars, the sensational nature of their newspapers grew, leading critics to dub the period, yellow journalism. The news was largely the same, but the tone was inflammatory. At its worse, yellow journalism included hoaxes, fake interviews, and personality reporting at the expense of accuracy (p. 291).

The event that most illustrates the tenor of the Pulitzer-Heart era known as yellow journalism was the coverage of the Spanish-American War, an abuse of the press to build circulation (Knowlton and Parsons, 1993, pp. 179-181). Nonetheless, some evidence suggests that both journalists were motivated by deeper desires to influence public policy for the good (Mander, 1982, p. 3).

In 1896 Hearst sent the dashing Richard Harding Davis to Cuba to cover the conflict between the Spanish authorities and the Cuban rebels, but Davis wired his boss that all was quiet. Hearst wired back: "You furnish the pictures and I'll furnish the war" (Schudson, 1978, p. 62). Covering the conflict was difficult at best and the reports, like any other war correspondence, were tainted by exaggeration, mistakes and misinformation. Among the problems was getting to the action. Many correspondents could not get food, so they had to hang back well behind the front and interview the wounded, many of whom were delirious (Mander, 1982, p. 2) and, therefore, unreliable. For Pulitzer and Hearst, the promotion of U. S. intervention resulted from a genuine desire to influence public policy, not much of a stretch for two men from an Emersonian tradition of the individual against the government (p. 3). Nonetheless, the coverage of the war made Hearst's *New York Journal* the more popular of the two newspapers (Riley, 1996, p. 292). In 1898, Spain granted Cuba its independence in the Treaty of Paris and ceded the Philippines, Guam, and Puerto Rico to the United States (Folkerts and Teeter, 1989, p. 274). Between 1898 and 1899 the United States annexed Wake Island, Hawaii, and Samoa but the Spanish-American War marked the culmination of the nation's desire to acquire additional land as a burgeoning empire (pp. 274-275).

Yellow journalism is considered a setback by Progressive School historians. They concentrate on the ideological conflict between the press and those in power who want to thwart freedom of speech. The Consensus school would evaluate the Hearst-Pulitzer performance as the nation united against a common foe and the role of the press to contribute to national unity. Perhaps the best way to understand the struggle for autonomy by the press in early America, and then the scramble for circulation in the nineteenth century, is the role of society on the press. Just as the first newspapers were products of a number of forces, including the need for commercial news in an environment that could not support large personnel and elaborate machines, the press of the Gilded Age was the result of cultural forces shaping it (Sloan and Startt, 1989, p. 37).

While Benjamin Day of the *New York Sun* and James Gordon Bennett of the *New York Herald* printed sensational content in the 1830s, Hearst and Pulitzer gave more attention to common life. The Bennett newspaper was the first to avoid entanglements with political parties (Schudson, 1978, p. 21) and include articles on sports, financial news, religion news, and other content that ordinary readers enjoyed. Shaw and Slater (1985) see little difference between the news of the 1830s and today. For example, the *Williamsport Sun-Gazette* published a humorous news story Monday, July 26, 1994, on a Williamsport clergyman who stopped a Sunday worship service to punch a parishioner who accused the minister of stealing. That article was featured on the front page of the newspaper and the Associated Press ran a similar story of its own on the incident. Is that content sensational? "Such news sold, still sells, and most likely will sell, where news is determined by the marketplace" (Shaw and Slater, 1985, p. 86). Yet Nerone (1987) found this kind of history faulty for using assumptions from today to analyze newspapers of earlier periods; changes in content are best understood as evolutionary–the result of the interaction of society and culture (p. 376).

Francke (1985) offered another view of the sensationalism of this period, noting that between the 1830s and 1880s, reporting techniques of documentary, observation, and interview evolved (p. 81). Reporters were not resorting to sensationalism in their prose, but borrowing techniques already used by others. For instance, court documents contained sensational details, and awaited reprinting in the popular form of a news report. Following Bennett's example, reporters questioned sources as police might do in an interrogation. In addition, police courts offered reporters the opportunity to provide eyewitness accounts in the form of observation; however, the backdrop for all these techniques are reporting the doings of a low-status world of prisons, slums and asylums. The context may have done more to plant the idea that the report relied on sensation for its appeal. In short, what was considered overly dramatic in the 1880s was the development of a reporting technique that applied the techniques of social science in an effort to reflect the reality of the mechanistic world, a practice that eventually led to standardization and the idea that all things can be measured (p. 84).

Beyond sensationalism of the late nineteenth century is the question of objectivity that dominates Schudson's *Discovering the News* (1978). Schudson referred to George Herbert Mead's idea of a newspaper's function to tell a story, not report facts (p. 89). The aesthetic function of providing enjoyable information helps readers "to interpret their own lives and to relate them to the nation, town, or class to which they belong" and to act "as a guide to living not so much by providing facts as by selecting them and framing them (Schudson, 1978, p. 89). Schiller (1981) said this ideological construct is a part of a stylized narrative that reflects the dominant social system's values (p. 1) and a cultural form that resonants with the broad consensus about the way things are (p. 2).

The grim city life was seen when reporter-photographer Jacob Riis wrote a best selling description of New York poverty with his *How the Other Half Lives* in 1890 (Bohlander, 1992, p. 14). In 1893 author Stephen Crane wrote his first novel on slum life, *Maggie: A Girl of the Streets*, but it offended publishers with its stark realism, forcing Crane to print it himself (Daniel, 1987, p. 15). By 1904, this kind of reality-reporting characterized the muckraking age with exposes such as Lincoln Steffens's *The Shame of the Cities*," articles that indicted government and business for corruption. By 1906, Upton Sinclair's famous expose on the meat-packing industry was released as *The Jungle,* and Ida Tarbell's series on Standard Oil Company ran in *McClure's* from 1902 until 1904 (Emery et al, 1996, pp. 226-228).

The rise of concepts such as objectivity, particularly in the early nineteenth century's Penny Press era, relied on a strong Judeo-Christian ethic to build their audiences outside the newsroom and reshape a value system inside the newsroom. This ethic also encouraged a positivistic world view that was adapted by newsrooms in the guise of a convention known as objectivity (Schudson, 1978, p. 76). For instance, the famous Robinson-Jewett's murder case of 1836 is an example of journalistic investigation that relied on the fact collecting of a police officer (Stephens, 1997, pp. 234-237). Editor James Gordon Bennett, Sr., of the *New York Herald* went to the scene of an ax murder of a prostitute named Ellen Jewett, reported the appearance of her bedroom, and conducted an interview with the housekeeper as a police officer might do, which is an early example of the formal interview. Richard P. Robinson, considered powerful and upper class, was arrested for the murder but was later acquitted for the crime. Later in the 1840s other New York newspapers launched a moral war against Bennett for his questionable content and readers boycotted the *Herald*, but by 1850 his style of journalism had made his newspaper the best selling daily in the nation with 30,000 copies daily (p. 239). Bennett's reporting of a murder story, now known as the crime story, drew a large audience who suspected that corruption of powerful people was pervasive (Folkerts and Teeter, 1989, pp. 237-238).

Regardless, the nineteenth century was the formative time in journalism. The reliance on attribution of sources to reduce the responsibility of reporters suggests the codification of news reporting (Schudson, 1978) that elevates world view to the place of a secular religion, where adherents must blindly obey or face the calumny of peers and superiors. The objectivity standard reluctantly embraced by some journalists yet today is rarely recognized by most of the press corps as a legitimate goal in news reporting but is the basis for criticism on coverage of racial issues, labor controversies, and religious rights. While Schiller and Schudson talk rather loosely about additional training of news reporters as a solution (Schiller, 1981, p. 194; Schudson, 1978, p. 152), the acceptance of objectivity as reality and news reports as snapshots of reality continues to be taught to journalists, who repeat the ritual generation after generation. Sheldon's experiment combined the informational model of staid journalism (Kielbowicz, 1996, p. 345), Ochs' approach, with Pulitzer, Hearst and Day's story model. Sheldon mixed in ample commentary and produced a newspaper very much in the tradition of advocacy journalism where the editor uses the news columns to express an opinion.

By 1835, Americans expected factual rather than partisan accounts in newspapers. For example, Richard Adams Locke's moon hoax in *The New York Sun* of 1835 was so convincing because it relied on the rhetoric of science (Schiller, 1981, pp. 77-80). The *Sun* reported that a huge telescope discovered new life forms on the moon that "averaged four feet in height, were covered, except on the face, with short and glossy copper-colored hair, and had wings composed of a thin membrane" (Stephens, 1997, p. 244). When the hoax was revealed, readers were alarmed but circulation continued to increase. The lower classes expected public enlightenment and value-free journalism, or, at least, reporting that did not reflect the values of the wealthy and power. For Schiller, this expectation of readers paved the way for acceptance of an objective universe and the rise of a single-science standard that explained the mechanisms of all life's activities. This widespread belief in the acceptance of a uniform, objective world helped contribute to notions of a democracy on the rise and hope in the public good.

A Supporter of the Reform Press

Beyond the public good, Wiebe (1967) found that the country was preoccupied with purity in the 1880s and tried to outlaw liquor (p. 56). Reform newspapers flourished throughout the 1800s. The women's movement, formally organized July 20, 1848, in Seneca Falls, New York, inspired a number of women's publications such as Amelia Bloomer's *Lily*, a temperance publication that evolved into part of the suffragist press (Folkerts and Teeter, 1989, p. 291). Susan B. Anthony began *The Revolution*, a weekly, in 1868 with Elizabeth Cady Stanton as editor (p. 293). In 1870 Lucy Stone and her husband Henry Blackwell began *Woman's Journal*, a publication that survived until 1917, shortly before passage of the suffrage amendment (p. 294).

In addition to publications reflecting the reform movement of women's voting rights were black newspapers. Of the 40 published between 1827 and 1865, Frederick Douglass's *The North Star* was read both in the United States and Europe (Emery et al, 1996, p. 127 129). Late in the nineteenth century, Booker T. Washington, president of Tuskegee Institute, "developed what became known as the Tuskegee Machine, a national network of editors and other influential black leaders loyal to Washington" (Folkerts and Teeter, 1989, p. 296). The black press, while vigorous, often failed from the financial and social strain of publishing (p. 297).

In some cases, reform movements were successful and borrowed from religious traditions to implement their goals. Spiritualism and pseudo-science were seen as solutions but Wiebe said most Americans looked for peace in Protestantism, "the most natural of all reservoirs of hope" (1967, p. 63). Some business reformers believed that by treating employees as brethren and holding discussion groups, mutual understanding would emerge. Most Americans at the time considered their country to be a nation of God and meant to prosper.

By the 1890s, reform movements had withered (p. 90). Labor was still restless, corporations with their monopolies still worried about a loss of control and political affiliation proved to be divisive in smaller communities, making for a pathological state of the nation. At this point in U. S. history, Wiebe identified the professionalization of groups such as medicine, education, and journalism, which resorted to use of the scientific method in reporting in an effort to appeal to the growing middle class (Wiebe, 1967, p. 120; Schudson, 1978, pp. 173-175). This middle class expected that the hidden hand of commerce of Adam Smith and David Ricardo would lead to utopia; meanwhile Social Gospellers and Christian Socialists, expected that the middle class would run the new order. The Progressive view of history gripped the country with the theme that progress was possible in stages. Evangelist Walter Rauschenbusch taught that the outcome of this progression would be to bring "society to the verge of Christ's commonwealth" (Wiebe, 1967, p. 143). By the turn of the century, however, the Christian tradition of God and the devil struggling for souls and the dualism of competition versus cooperation was replaced with a bureaucratic orientation and the idea of society working as an efficient machine. This kind of thinking still relied on faith, but faith in scientific method where freedom would lead to pure, rational democracy.

Reporters of the era tended to share admiration for scientific discipline, supporting the Jacksonian idea of democracy along with the idea that systematic, detached data collection is available to all. Quoting Clarence Darrow, Schudson wrote, "The world has grown tired of preachers and sermons; today it asks for facts. It has grown tired of fairies and angels, and asks for flesh and blood" (1978, p. 73). Empirical inquiry was part of the democratic vision, not religion. Yet Americans were not ready to abandon the trappings of a religious system filled with sin, worship, and morality. In journalism, elite newspapers such as *The New York Times* fulfilled that desire for something superior, expressed by a Times supporter who said, "It is in the Times that we can all worship the Idols of the Cave without being caught in our idolatry" (Schudson, 1978, p. 116).

A Supporter of Commentary

By the late nineteenth century, two ideals of reporting clashed. The educated classes wanted information, but the lower classes wanted a good story in the tradition of the Realists, those reporters-turned-novelists such as Jack London, Theodore Dreiser, Stephen Crane, Frank Norris and Willa Cather. Without the support of political parties, the Penny Press depended on advertising and street sales, not subscriptions, for its subsidies. Schudson (1978) argued that the Penny Press invoked advertising to benefit itself by promoting a newspaper's exclusive coverage while the more respectable newspapers such as *The New York Times* appealed to decency (p. 118). The choice of newspapers had a moral dimension, with the *Times* receiving social approval, which can be associated with rationality and control over one's life. Schudson argued that the upper classes identified with *The Times* and a sense of self-denial while the lower classes preferred the self indulgent model of the Penny Press with its news articles heavy on entertainment value.

By the twilight of the nineteenth century, newspapers thrived as commercial institutions that used display advertising for the bulk of their capital (Folkerts and Teeter, 1989, p. 284). The newspapers that grew relied on evening sales because advertisers thought women, the readers most likely to be the purchasers in the home, would spend more time with the publication. While some publications gained attention with single social or political campaign issues such as women's voting rights, the newspapers that sought a general circulation audience fared the best. Niche newspapers could not attract the steady support and advertising that a publication needed to remain vibrant. To satisfy the audience's desire for a variety of content, publishers utilized Ochs's information model or Hearst-Pulitzer's crusade-sensational story model. By 1900, Sheldon sensed that the public's appetite for newspapers that intruded into the private lives of sources was not the kind of journalism that Jesus would practice. When Sheldon's opportunity arrived, he used his week as editor to move beyond mere criticism of the sensational press and his right to freedom of the press; he presented some of the same content found in the reform press, but with an attempt to influence all the readers of the mainstream press.

By the time Sheldon became editor of *The Topeka Daily Capital* for a week in March 1900, readers of the mainstream press considered sports and crime as standard news, two departments that Sheldon downplayed in his Sheldon edition. One of the most exciting murders of the day was a case of Mrs. Luetgers, murdered by her husband, a sausage manufacturer. Historian Mott wrote that Mr. Luetger "was accused of cutting up his wife's body, placing it in the vats of his manufactory, and boiling it in a potash solution" (1941, p. 578). Sheldon refused to print this kind of lurid detail and used a suicide of a senator's son to present tragic news with sensitivity (Sheldon, 1925, p. 132). "I see nothing to be gained by relating the ghastly details of human frailty and sin," Sheldon wrote in his autobiography (1925, p. 132).

In sports, the famous Corbett-Fitzsimmons boxing match in Nevada City in 1897 dominated sports headlines. Fitzsimmons won by knocking out Corbett with a blow to the solar plexus. By this time in newspaper development, the sports page had become a department of its own. Wireless communication was used for the first time with sports in 1899 with international yacht races (Mott, 1941, p. 579).

The editorial pages, rather than the news pages, gained prominence during Sheldon's time as editor. "The editorials themselves were not long, and never hard to read," wrote historian Frank Luther Mott of this period (p. 581). The style then, as now, was to keep the ideas simple. Sheldon practiced this convention as editor in writing about Prohibition, the Kingdom of God, and the characteristics of a Christian daily newspaper. His standard for journalism was to permit commentary to dominate news.

One of the controversies of the press during Sheldon's era was the role of Sunday editions. Following the Spanish-American War of 1898, Sunday newspapers proliferated (p. 584). While some denominations attempted to have laws passed to restrict Sunday newspapers from circulating, the Sunday newspapers continued to flourish. For instance, before the turn of the century, the *Chicago Tribune* was publishing 60 pages of copy in its Sunday newspaper. In addition, colored supplements for newspapers became popular. The political cartoon spread widely between 1892 and 1895, particularly for the Sunday editions (p. 587). The free silver controversy over a monetary standard during the 1896 McKinley–Bryan presidential election led to the prolific use of political cartoons.

By the 1880s, the first photographs began appearing in the press (Stephens, 1997, p. 269); however, Sheldon's newspaper did not use photographs during his reign as editor in 1900. Sheldon's edition relied on line-cut drawings for illustrations for both the news and advertising pages.

For Sheldon, however, the newspaper that he wanted to fashion would be directive using Christian morality. Sheldon told graduates of Washburn College in 1899, the year before Sheldon's newspaper experiment ("New Opportunities," 1899, pp. 24-26):

> What more tremendous career could a man or woman
> ask than to go into some town where sin ruled, and
> begin a paper that stood up for law, and temperance,
> and righteousness in business, and Brotherhood, and
> nonsectarianism in religion, and nonpartisanship in
> politics and Christianity at the core of every
> transaction between man and man, and see that paper
> have an influence in making old things all over?

In that speech, Sheldon went on to urge some of the graduates to enter journalism to transform it and to work with the church "as the means by which Christian principle shall be applied to every human condition and the cause of God's Kingdom shall be advanced because men will then believe the prayer they now offer, 'Thy will be done in earth as it is in heaven'" ("New opportunities," 1899, pp. 24-26). For Sheldon, the journalism that he wanted to practice was not so far removed from the long-established traditions of the American press. The *New England Courant* wanted to be a voice of opposition against the dominant power while attempting to ignite thought over religion. It challenged the Puritan dominated *Boston Gazette.* Sheldon's experiment was no different; he wanted to challenge the dominant order and make readers think, but along the lines that Sheldon thought. In the next chapter, this vision that Sheldon proposed is explored. In sum, Sheldon would permit a reader to respond personally to his convictions, but only after that person followed Sheldon's very specific and very narrow prescription for life by responding to the question, "What would Jesus do?"

By late twentieth century standards, critics could dismiss Sheldon's experiment as another example of traditional journalism where a publisher took a vigorous viewpoint but failed to present detailed news coverage. Yet the day following the experiment, March 18, 1900, William Allen White, a fellow Kansan and leader of the *Emporia Gazette* wrote that Sheldon's newspaper caused readers to think and awakened in journalists ideas on making a daily newspaper cleaner (Ripley, 1965, p. 37). Sheldon wanted a clean newspaper, and he predicted in 1896 that this kind of newspaper likely would be dull because it would not dwell on the graphic details of crime reports and other news such as sports (Ripley, 1968, p. 248). When given a chance to model the ideal, Sheldon's newspaper avoided the conflict that Hearst and Pulitzer savored in their news coverage, adopting instead an approach more like Ochs's information model but with far less lively content. In chapter six, a more complete picture of Sheldon's vision of Christian journalism is explored, particularly from his six editorials. The editorials along with the news and advertisements that he published the week of March 13, 1900 reveal Sheldon's model for the Christian newspaper. In the process, Sheldon also revealed the rhetorical vision that he wanted all who are engaged in the experiment to possess.

Summary

Sheldon followed in the tradition of personal editors who expressed a personal vision in the news and editorial pages of their general-circulation newspapers. Sheldon advocated reform and challenged the ruling elites and the status quo, a convention that dates back to colonial period journalism. His newspaper was not bound to a Christian denomination as was the Puritan-dominated *Boston Gazette* in the eighteenth century, but he favored a Christian worldview as the organizing ideology for his publication. Sheldon tried to apply the biblical idea of avoiding gossip in news coverage but succeeded in producing vague news accounts that prompted many of his readers to obtain the *Topeka State Journal*, the evening competition, to learn the news of the day. In the name of propriety, Sheldon would make a general statement about leaders lying about their taxes (Sheldon, 1900k, p. 1), but not identify the accused specifically. In the process, he inadvertently condemned all leaders. Meanwhile, the *Topeka State Journal* provided a list that identified specific individuals and the taxes they owed as established by the tax office. That type of reporting, known as precision journalism, is recognized as high-quality writing (Olasky, 1996).

Nonetheless, Sheldon succeeded in offering an alternative to the sensational journalism of the day that tended to present news to inflame reader's emotions. In addition, his newspaper served the goals of the reform movement and tried to improve the lot of ordinary readers. However, Sheldon's newspaper became dominated with the issue of temperance and deviated from the expectations of a mainstream newspaper that was meant to be read by a heterogeneous audience with a variety of political, economic and religious beliefs. While the content of Sheldon's newspaper was valuable, it focused too narrowly on Sheldon's social agenda, particularly temperance, and failed to give the readers the news of the day that answered the basic questions of who did what to whom and why.

Chapter 7

Did Newspapers Report Religion in Sheldon's Day?

Nationally syndicated religion columnist Terry Mattingly recalls an editor at *The Charlotte Observer* in North Carolina who would not pursue coverage of national religion that focused on denominational schisms because, he said, "Every time you write about that stuff we get too many letters to the editor" (Personal Communication, October 26, 2001). Information with impact is usually the quality that makes news all the more vital. That certainly was the case of news and religion in colonial America, and a parallel persists today, despite the concern of Mattingly's editor.

In colonial America, clergy disseminated news about the world and the proper reaction to it (Silk, 1995, p. 10). Today journalists fulfill that role, but it is rare for a news reporter to do what the early America clergy did–interpret the day's events from a Christian perspective.

Defining Christian Journalism

The term Christian journalism is ambiguous and can mean sanctified secularism, strident propaganda or something else entirely (Hoover, 1989, p. 29). For Charles Sheldon's Congregationalists in American in 1894, Christian journalism meant more than the mere grafting Christian content into newspaper content. For journalists who are activists, Christian journalism means more than the mere grafting onto the secular content of newspapers religious principles and aims. Christian journalism can be defined as advocacy journalism where the redemption message is a central feature of the news and editorials.

Some vestige of this kind of journalism can be found throughout the history of the press, but it was most common during the nineteenth century. Today it is best represented by *World* magazine that seeks to present news "to see what God is doing today" (Olasky, 1988, p. 70). Tragic news can show the consequences of sin while non-tragic news can show God's favor, according to the *World* model.

Mattingly rejects this definition of Christian journalism, noting that Olasky's approach to journalism borrows from a European model: "A classically European model in which media admit their subjectivity and advocate specific viewpoints. Ironically, while this approach is usually identified with overtly progressive publications, or covertly progressive mainstream media, Olasky's 'directed reporting' concept offers a conservative Christian version of this approach." Both Mattingly and Olasky appear to agree that the church press that promotes institutional goals and causes is a public relations effort, not journalism. For others, a definition of Christian journalism today is as unwieldy as a definition of religious journalism (Hoover, 1989, p. 29). For purposes of this work, "Christian journalism" will be the term used to mean the journalism produced by a Christian to promote Christianity.

Christian Journalism in Colonial America

Christian journalism was not labeled as such in colonial America, but existed as the information circulated as news. Today this kind of writing would be known as advocacy journalism. In that day, news was linked to an appreciation of the role of the divine in ordinary affairs as a given, hence the regular appeals by seventeenth and eighteenth century editors for "a day of solemn fast, prayer, and humiliation before Almighty God" (Copeland, 1995, p. 10). The colonial period did not have organizations committed exclusively to perception management, e. g. public relations, but the news writing could be thought of as part of a public relations program because of the blending of news and boorsterism.

The notion of objectivity , where opinion is said to be eliminated from the newspaper prose, was not linked with journalism until the early twentieth century (Schudson, 1978).[6] Thus, even the idea of systematic news collection was not yet established; nonetheless, newspapers on both sides of the Atlantic flourished. They presented their news from a subjective viewpoint and found a ready audience.

---

[6] In more recent decades, the notion of objectivity has faded as an ideal that is achievable. These days newsrooms talk of fairness, the notion of identify all the stakeholders in a conflict and giving them an opportunity to comment on the issue.

As early as 1643, the crown used the law to attempt to control the press. The British Parliament passed a law restricting the sale of newsbooks to stop criticism of the rulers (Olasky, 1991, p. 17), which sparked additional controversy over the idea of equality under the law, a biblical idea. At least one Puritan critic, Alexander Leighton, wrote that the Bible was above every authority, including kings. Because of the principles suggested by the Bible, a king's subjects could evaluate the king's leadership along with anyone else against biblical standards (Olasky, 1996, p. 57). Despite laws against criticism, writers continued to publish news and measured the rulers using biblical arguments to support these positions. In the days of the Reformation, the doctrine of *sola scriptura* or "scripture alone" challenged Protestants to read their Bibles and write their objections to governmental abuses based on their understanding of Scripture. This practice reinforced the convention of mixing news with opinion in the newspapers of the period.

In the seventeenth century, the religious culture of the New England colonies influenced the characteristics of news (Nord, 1990, p. 10). According to Nord, news was defined as drawing on the collective past intermingled with the present and the future and subject to public meaning, a product of political, social and economic power. The people in seventeenth-century New England believed that everything occurred according to God's perfect plan, making news teleological. "The teleological order was not only divine but patterned, recurrent, meaningful, and intelligible" (Nord, 1990, p. 10). The content of news during this period between 1630 and 1730 was public in its importance but directed at the individual, reflecting an awareness of a personal response not only for one's actions, but also one's relationship with the divine. By the eighteenth century, newspapers began to distinguish between "news that is important (stories of public action) and news that is merely interesting (stories of unusual private occurrences)" (Nord, 1990, p. 10).

To illustrate his point, Nord recounted the October 17, 1637, birth of a monstrous baby to Mary Dyer, a follower of Anne Hutchinson, as published in 1644. The baby's condition isn't described but the account was written to suggest God was punishing the mother and her child for abandoning the Puritan faith. The governor of Massachusetts wrote much of the report to reveal "the designing hand of God and a message for the commonwealth of Massachusetts" (Nord, 1990, p. 11). The birth of Mary Dyer's deformed baby was viewed as evidence that God opposed the heretic Hutchinson. The event had public meaning and indicated divine providence, a theme that is repeated in Puritan theology and sociology. Since New England is the location of the first newspapers in America, this emphasis on divine providence is a basic ingredient in understanding the development of newspaper conventions.

In 1675, clergyman Increase Mather supported the Boston press and used events to provide meaning for readers (p. 21). Between 1688 and 1691, he turned his pen to political topics, but the undercurrent in his prose was that God had a special place in history for New England. Within this type of news were the conventions of reportorial empiricism and authoritative interpretation (p. 26). Reportorial empiricism, the collection of facts, was introduced in this period and has hence become the standard methodology of news reporting today. Also popular as news content was a review of a recent sermon, news of a church service, and the results of fasting, prayer and thanksgiving (pp. 7-10). Closely associated with this content was news of natural disasters, such as earthquakes that served as warnings to readers, or accounts of God's supply, such as the hungry family that found a pair of doves for dinner (p. 11). Copeland found: "Religion was vital to the lives of most colonial citizens, and newspapers provided reports of religious controversy and presented news tinted by religious belief throughout the colonial period" (1995, p. 26).

Christian Journalism in General Circulation Newspapers

Mott (1941) called the nineteenth century the beginning of the Protestant press and the era of 1801 to 1833 as the time of the religious newspaper, "a weekly journal which mingled secular news and religious miscellany ..." (p. 206). Among the nearly 100 religious newspapers were the *Congregational Recorder* in Boston and the *Episcopal Recorder* in Philadelphia, but most of this press failed or was transformed into newspapers crusading for a cause such as abolition. By the 1860s, the religious press became almost exclusively denominational (p. 322). In the summer of 1860, the *New York Sun* was sold to a publisher named Morrison who practiced a kind of Christian journalism, according to Mott. "Morrison saw to it that a prayer meeting was held everyday at noon in the Sun editorial rooms; and after the (Civil) War had begun, he urged that Union generals should be instructed not to fight battles on Sundays" (p. 373). By the end of 1861, Morrison's interest in religious meetings and missionaries had waned, and the newspaper returned to the content of the other New York newspapers. The impact of the Great Revival of 1858 may have influenced Morrison at first, but Mott does not cite any reasons for Morrison abandoning this "mildly evangelical journalism" content (1941, p. 373).

Two other newspapers tried a similar approach with little success. *The New York Daily Witness* tried to be a religious daily but only lasted from 1871 to 1879, and the *Boston Daily News*, begun in 1869, aspired to be a moral, religious daily but failed in 1876.

In a development related to religious newspapers or Christian journalism, Silk (1995) found that in the early nineteenth century a desire to print inexpensive Bibles helped transform the publishing industry and influenced Christian journalism. Mass media in America is tied to the tract and Bible movements of the 1820s because evangelical Christian publicists wanted "to deliver the same printed message to everyone in America" (Nord, 1984, p. 2). While evangelicals had long used printing to spread the Gospel, it was the intensity of the desire to spread the message that was new in the 1820s (p. 3). During this period, the United States was threatened by the arguments that challenged orthodox religion. Thomas Paine's *Age of Reason,* a book that celebrated reason alone as the governing approach to life, was sold for less than 2 cents a copy and men such as Federalist Elias Boudinot resolved to counteract this philosophy with a godly influence. Boudinot joined forces with the Rev. Jedidiah Morse to organize private associations to spread the gospel through tracts (p. 4). Both men were conservatives and believers in tradition. Each feared liberal Christianity and mourned the decline of Federalism and Calvinism.

New Haven was the first important American tract society and was established in 1807. This society and many others recognized a need for a national effort and the cooperation of denominations. The British Religious Tract Society, founded in London in 1799, was among the contributors to the America tract movement (p. 5), and actually the overseas link was stronger than the link to the American communities. To avoid denominational friction, the British suggested these societies seek a common denominator. Many of the tracts contained either narratives of conversion experiences or widely acceptable conservative Christian doctrines. The American tract societies modeled their tracts after the British, but found it difficult to finance the mass printing and distribution of the work (p. 6). To economize, the societies promoted new printing techniques and inexpensive papermaking (p. 7). New York of the 1810s and 1820s was the best place to appreciate the rewards of a thriving economy and printing revolution. A process of stereotyping was among the first innovations where a movable type could be set as a solid page and be used again and again (p. 8). This process proved thrifty for big jobs. The first book stereotyped in the United States was John Watts's catechism in 1813. The American Bible

Society used stereotyping in 1820 to become a leading American book publisher (p. 9). By 1825, the smaller tract societies merged to become the American Tract Society and used New York as their headquarters.

The tract societies then invested in steam-powered presses, which made the production of tracts even more inexpensive (p. 10). Daniel Treadwell's steam-powered press, an intermediate press, was better than a hand press and was much faster. The American Tract Society used the Treadwell press in 1826 (p. 11). Another innovation was cheaper papermaking. French inventor Nicholas-Louis Robert created a papermaking machine in the late 1790s that led to a cut in the cost of paper by 60%.

By the late 1820s, the tract and Bible societies felt prepared to saturate the nation with the message (p. 12). The organizers of the society offered to put aside denominational issues to support the work of evangelism (p. 12). To this end, the Bible would be published without a note or a comment. Before long, the work of printing centralize in New York (p. 15) drew on the wealth there, including the benevolence of Arthur Tappan, an import trader who generously supported the American Tract Society (p. 16). In May 1829, the Rev. James Milnor, speaking for the board of the American Bible Society, said that the society would supply a Bible to every family in the United States that needed one (p. 18). The goal proved unattainable, but more than a million inexpensive Bibles and ten million tracts were distributed (Silk, 1995, p. 17). By 1835, the centralized and systematic publication of tracts as mass media was a reality. Although these developments are not part of newspaper publishing per se, the motivation behind them is of note to understand the great interest in printing as a way to galvanize faith.

Silk asserts that the nineteenth-century newspapers did not practice Christian journalism until the *Boston Recorder* was founded in 1816 (1995, p. 16). Olasky (1990) claims that the contents of the *Boston Recorder* relied on what he called a macro-story, "a central idea that overarches the daily bits and pieces of journalistic coverage" (p. 19). This central idea was published news that showed theological truth impeded in ordinary news reports (p. 21). Editor Nathaniel Willis published his newspaper to emphasize inhumanity, as seen in the burning of a slave (p. 22). He also published an account of a murderer who believed his sins were too numerous to be pardoned. According to his autobiography published in Hudson (1968), Willis went to a revival in November 1807 when he was 27 and learned that Christ was his savior. In the following months, he sold the politically-inspired newspaper with which he has worked, tried to make a living in the grocery business, and began publishing a Christian newspaper on January 3, 1816 (pp. 291-292). In the mid-1830s, Willis turned over leadership of his newspaper to others, and the macro-story changed from an emphasis on man's sinfulness to news for news's sake.

In 1846, John Redpath Dougall began a weekly newspaper with a Christian identity in Canada (Dougall, 1900, p. 1). Writing for Charles Sheldon's Jesus newspaper on March 17, 1900, Dougall describes the history of his newspaper as an "advocate of evangelical religion and Puritan morals, including an uncompromising demand for the prohibition of the liquor trade. In religion it eschewed all denominationalism; in politics it was absolutely free of party trammel" (Dougall, 1900, p. 1). By 1860, his newspaper, the *Montreal Daily Witness*, had became a daily publication. Dougall states that his newspaper contained political news and opinion but marked its distinction, in particular, by examining advertising claims and accepting only legitimate products. "The Christian journalist must be prepared for martyrdom just as the Christian who is true to any other calling must be," wrote Dougall in refusing questionable advertising (1900, p. 1).

Denominational Newspapers in the Nineteenth century

Instead of general-circulation newspapers that practiced Christian journalism, denominational newspapers followed *Willis's Recorder* as part of an explosion of Christian publishing in the early nineteenth century "that amounted to the invention of the mass media in America" (Silk, 1995, p. 16). By 1872, between 330 and 340 religious newspapers were published in the United States (p. 30).

In the early nineteenth century, newspapers with a Christian or religious identification were common. John Andrews's *Weekly Recorder*, the first Christian newspaper of the Northwest, began in 1814 and was designed to perform very ordinary secular functions while compensating for the shortage of religious personnel in reaching a scattered population in support of Christian orthodoxy in belief and practice. Sometimes denominations worked together on a publication as was the case of the *Delaware Gazette and Religious Informer*, the work of Presbyterians and Baptists in Ohio. Christians often combined labors because each group lacked a critical mass to keep a publication viable.

By the 1840s, a religious newspaper typically circulated once a week with separate editorial departments (p. 4). The front page contained news of theology, morality, literature, and other classical topics such as science and history. The second page was reserved for opinion, correspondence, and news of church or denominational activities. In addition, this section included news on revivals and

Sunday schools. The third page contained foreign, national, and local news and advertisements. The last page also carried advertisements and sometimes included poetry and miscellaneous information, such as frontier superstitions or columns on food processing (p. 5). Headings for temperance, slavery, and other reform issues appeared anywhere in the typical publication.

Religious newspapers often were associated with schools; one example was the *Lutheran Standard*, begun in 1842 with staff from Capital University in Columbus, Ohio (p. 12). Whether sponsored by a school or a denomination, these newspapers often lost money and those that did become solvent often had to utilize the resources of a denomination. For instance, the General Conference of the Methodist Episcopal Church sponsored not only the *Western Christian Advocate* of Cincinnati from 1834 until it ceased in 1939, but also the *Northwestern Christian Advocate* of Chicago, in print from 1853 until 1939 (p. 10). The General Conference of the United Brethren published the *Religious Telescope* from 1835 to 1946, a publication founded in 1831 by the Roman Catholics in Cincinnati as an authorized diocesan publication. It initially succeeded but endured financial instability in 1852 when the publisher warned the church that further debt would lead to the suspension of the *Telegraph* much to the great joy of all the opponents. Denominational newspapers relied on paid subscriptions and attempted to inspire readers to support publications with the same zeal that fired an editor to his calling (p. 15). Nonetheless, many readers subscribed on credit and failed to pay, leading the same zealous editors to complain bitterly in print of shameful credit practices (p. 17). Despite unpaid subscriptions, newspapers usually continued to be delivered with some subscribers owing a balance of $12 when subscriptions cost about $1.50 annually. Some editors published a list of those subscribers in arrears, but editors and proprietors simply would not dilute their religious mission by giving up subscribers in order to relieve financial strain.

Newspapers used paid advertising but banned liquor and tobacco content as well as advertisements for theaters and horse races (p. 21). Patent medicines, a great source of advertising revenue, were treated differently by different publications. The *Baptist Christian Register* criticized patent medicine advertising, saying that the seller of these products deceives society, ruins health, and accumulates a fortune.

While religious publications promised much in the way of enlightenment, most failed because they lacked sufficient numbers of readers (Nerone, 1989). Furthermore, these publications often were operated by an elite who wanted the publication to reflect their values.

The magazines that did succeed tapped into the built-in readership of a denomination. Protestant publications used their pages to criticize Catholicism under the guise of religious discussion. In addition, the Protestant press invoked "the symbols of America's free democratic institutions to characterize their own religious institutions (Nerone, 1989, p. 192.) For instance, one Protestant publication compared Catholicism to unenlightened monarchism; but this approach, presented as free enquiry, amounted to strident propaganda.

Nerone (1989) noted that in the 1830s the religious periodicals that succeeded were connected to organizations and became devoted to the religious organization, not scientific enquiry; although these editors believed that free scientific investigation of religion would lead to popular enlightenment. The leaders of the religious press professed a belief in the discoverable religious truth and scientific investigation, furthermore, the press was seen as the vehicle to spread this kind of enlightenment.

To build audiences, many of these publications resorted to sentiment and later sensationalism publishing sermon-like essays rather than news. These periodicals avoided advertising and relied on support of like-minded readers, who often did not deliver, leading to a periodical's demise. Literary publications succeeded in Cincinnati, but only when they exploited popular attitudes (Nerone, 1989). Nerone did not read economics into the explanation for success and failure. Some publications survived because their content was accepted by readers, but regardless of how the publications fared, Nerone said those interested in serious western literature were persistent out of a belief that the rational reader wanted to be enlightened rather than entertained. The formula for success,, then was to reinforce "religious, moral and social attitudes rather than reshape them" (Nerone, 1989, p. 227).

The editor of the religious newspaper of the mid-nineteenth century was often the personality of the publication, often attracted to the work out of a duty to spread the Gospel. However, the chore of publishing and the complaints from readers and others associated with publishing left many editors unprepared for the hardship. Most of the editors of these newspapers were clergymen who shared a common expectation that newspapers were the most promising medium to communicate the Gospel to a wide audience (pp. 25-26). Among the number was the Rev. J. R. McDowall, editor of the *New York monthly*, McDowall's Journal. His motto was, "The world is our field and prevention is our aim." In August, 1834, McDowall argued that the Bible teaches the need to expose sin (Olasky, 1996, pp. 255-261). McDowall used Isaiah 58:1, "Show my people their transgressions and the house of Jacob their sins," and other scriptures to support his idea that journalists are on bibically solid ground when they write about vice and this contribution will be among the greatest any journalist can perform for his or her community.

Christian Journalism in the Nineteenth Century

In the mainstream press, Christianity was a factor, but not the raison d'etre. When Benjamin Day began his *New York Sun* in 1833, he installed as editor George W. Wisner, a journalist well known for his work in Christian newspapers (Olasky, 1991. p. 66). While the content of the *Sun* did not contain overtly Christian content, it emphasized news that demonstrated the ills of man such as crime, even adultery. In 1836, James Gordon Bennett said his *New York Herald* would do the same because he had seen human depravity to the core (p. 67).

While newspapers did not endorse a Christian doctrine, publishers were not above using the lexicon of faith to praise their newspapers. An editor during the Penny Press era of 1831 to 1861, Bennett said a newspaper "can send more souls to heaven, and save more from hell, than all of the churches or chapels in New York, beside making money at the same time" (Pratte, 1993, p. 1).

More typical of Christian content in mainstream newspapers was confined to the editorial page. In 1846, Horace Greeley and his *New York Tribune* squared off against Henry J. Raymond and his *New York Courier and Enquirer*. Greeley supported ideas to revolutionize society in order to create a truly fair America and embraced a number of causes known as communes, sometimes called associations. Among the associations was one supported by Albert Brisbane, a follower of Fourierism utopia socialism (p. 67), who considered a form of collective living known as associationism–communes to be a cure for reckless capitalism (Emery et al, 1996, p. 108). Brisbane sometimes wrote approvingly of religion but he scorned clergy, particularly Protestant ones, and argued that Nero was the most admirable figure in history, not Christ (Pratte, 1993, p. 7). Greeley embraced any ideas that offered solutions to a nation becoming increasingly industrial and plagued with urban problems (Emery et al, 1996, p. 107).

Raymond was Greeley's assistant editor before moving to *the New York Courier and Enquirer*. In 1851 Raymond began *The New York Daily Times*, later to be known as *The New York Times* (p. 109). In addition to his reputation as an orator, Raymond was a Presbyterian (Olasky, 1991, p. 70). In a series of 12 articles written between November 20, 1845, to April 28, 1846, Greeley and Raymond debated issues of political economy. When Greeley called on personal reform from societal reform, Raymond argued the reverse, noting that through

Christianity social progress can be made (p. 72). Greeley argued that once society's leaders changed, the rank-and-file would change as well, an argument that Olasky considered the ideology of the Social Gospel that enthralled turn-of-the-century clergy. However, Raymond's ideas were not far from the notion that society could be transformed; they highlighted the regular work of churches to relieve poverty and suffering (p. 73). Nonetheless, Raymond's debate rested on spiritual poverty leading to material poverty. Raymond said Greeley wrote as if he endorsed Christianity as the solution to the nation's woes but denied the doctrines of the Bible (p. 75). Raymond concluded in his twelfth article that the principles of true reform come from Heaven and the Christian religion is the only power that can reform society (p. 77).

In New York, newspapers during the Penny Press era contributed to reform in ways slightly different from the conventional sense of the word. Hoffert (1993) found that the *New York Daily Herald, The New York Daily Times* and the *New York Daily Tribune*, the largest newspapers of the day in the United States, covered extensively the conventions of woman's rights activists (p. 662). While the coverage was a mixture, with the *Herald* opposing the demands for women's rights, and the *Tribune* vacillating, the cumulative effect was that these newspapers gave women activists a forum to influence public opinion (Hoffert, 1993, p. 662).

During this period, others published distinctly Christian newspapers, such as Elijah Lovejoy who began the *St. Louis Observer* in 1834; however, this newspaper and the ones that followed it were consumed with abolitionist arguments (pp. 83-84). In 1845, Cassius Clay published the *True American*, another abolitionist newspaper, which called for salvation through grace and argued that when Christianity prevailed, earth would become like heaven (p. 85).

Religion as a department in a newspaper in the nineteenth century began with James Gordon Bennett and his *New York Herald* (Buddenbaum, 1987, p. 55; Hudson, 1968, p. 453). As an enterprising businessman, Bennett cultivated coverage of religion (Emery et al,, 1996, pp. 103-104) because "religion was something that people cared about and talked about, and it was also a content area that would let him tap a previously neglected audience" (Buddenbaum, 1987, p. 55). In 1840, other New York newspapers tried to portray Bennett's *Herald* as immoral for language such as "leg" instead of "limb" during a period known as the (Mott, 1941, p. 232). The Moral War amounted to New York newspapers singling out the *Herald* for its "immorality." Even clergy and the religious press criticized Bennett's newspaper for including coverage of news such as church meetings (Hudson, 1968, p.

453). Buddenbaum concluded from a content analysis of Bennett's *New York Herald* that its religion coverage changed from 1836 to 1844, and included neutral and positive reports on religion as well as satirical assaults. Bennett's religion coverage could be characterized as "old-style Christianity that emphasized personal morality and community over new Protestantism that seemed to equate true Christianity with money and empire" (Buddenbaum, 1987, p. 64).

Nonetheless, Bennett's coverage of an annual meeting of the Bible Society or of news linking religion with fiscal or sexual improprieties did much to attract readers, many of whom were from the lower economic class audience (pp. 63-64). Readers came to expect coverage of a religious event, but the more pious in the audience found fault with the press advertising tobacco, saloons, and theaters (Silk, 1995, p. 18). Among the most objectionable practices, as seen by the starchy Christian leaders of the day, was the success of the Sunday editions in the 1880s. As late as 1890, nearly 30 years after the Penny Press era, Dickens-Garcia (1989) found evidence that newspapers considered Sunday editions a distraction to the spiritual life of the community. The influence of the mass revival movement of the Second Great Awakening could still be felt. Dickens-Garcia (1989) found that the public "objected to newspapers' taking people's minds off spiritual matters, to work being conducted on the Sabbath, and to noisy hawking of papers on a day meant for serenity and worship" (p. 126).

Although James Gordon Bennett attempted a Sunday newspaper in 1835, he had to discontinue it because of opposition from clergy and others in the defense of the sacredness of the day of rest. Bennett managed to establish his *New York Sunday Herald* in 1841 around the height of the Penny Press days, and it was one of the few to endure. Buddenbaum (1987) found that Bennett relied on the appeal of religion to build his audience (p. 55), his circulation, and his profits; and he used religion content to counter the Moral War waged against his newspaper by the other New York giants.

In the South, newspapers treated religion and spiritualism with particular care. Delp (1985) notes that in the years preceding the Civil War, southern newspapers were cautious about religious movements and ideas originating from the North that might threaten the practice of slavery. Slavery aside, spiritualism such as animal magnetism was seen as a threat to Christianity. Although some in the South noted interest in spiritualism, the established churches "mounted a theological crusade aimed at spiritualism which it feared had inundated the North and was now flowing southward" (Delp, 1985, p. 93). Southern secessionists capitalized on the fear of spiritualism, using it for its propaganda value in fomenting public opinion in the South for war.

Religion coverage continued throughout the century, often utilizing the revival for its variety of human-interest angles. During a mini-awakening of 1857-1858, Horace Greeley's *New York Tribune* devoted an entire issue to a revival led by Charles Finney, who later praised Greeley for helping with the work of the revival by virtue of the *Tribune*'s coverage (p. 20). However, by the end of the century, crusades rarely made the front page. Instead, the 1870s found general-circulation newspapers publishing a page of announcements for church events and syndicated features such as the International Sunday School Lesson (p. 25).

Economics and Secularism

In the Midwest in the nineteenth century, newspapers were apt to emphasize enlightenment (Nerone, 1989, p. 100); however, news and opinions became marketable commodities (p. 286). Enlightenment, once a noble pursuit, was redefined by organizations such as political parties and religions to be a self-serving truth (p. 286). These truths concerned politics, what Nerone calls the truths of "the professional organizational elite" (1989, p. 287). "This triumph of Democracy seemed illusory to those who took seriously the promise of enlightenment. A sense of betrayal has ever since been the birthright of the American utopian" (Nerone, 1989, p. 287).

News content is parallel to a product or a commodity that can be created and sold (Baldasty, 1992, p. 140). When the republic was young, this commodity was used to win political contest, but with the rise of business, the advocates of politics became the advocates of business. Where once news meant voters, now news meant consumers (p. 144), the "business imperative" (Baldasty, 1992, p. 99).

In the 1830s, just when the party patronage began to dry up and the readers' fascination with all things political was waning, newspapers turned from political patronage to another form of subsidy: advertising revenue. While self-promotion by political candidates was once thought to be impolite, this prohibition softened and candidates did speak for themselves, circumventing the need for a party press and its propaganda function. As newspapers became more unaffiliated with political parties and the urban press expanded to larger audiences, the press became market driven.

Between the years of 1879 and 1899, subscription rates went from 56% of a newspaper's income to 44%, while advertising rates went from 44% to 56% (Baldasty, 1992). With more emphasis on advertising income, newspapers began courting advertisers and disguised paid advertising as news. News was redefined to delete references to companies when the news might unduly harm the business's reputation, as in the case of a fire in a cigar factory. Good newspapers were publications that accommodated advertisers.

To compete in this business environment, the strategy became: Keep operating expenses low. Reporters earned their pay by writing by the column inch of newspaper copy, forcing some reporters to write a dozen articles a day or. In one case newspaper legend H. L. Mencken once fabricated a story on a drowning. Newspapers purchased partially completed newspapers called "patents inside" and "patents outside" to cut down on the expense of collecting news (Baldasty, 1992, p. 91-92). With these partially completed newspapers, publishers could add articles of their own and give the appearance of a full newspaper. The beat system of assigning reporters to report on organizations most likely to have information processed and ready to print became the standard practice of news collecting; in addition, newspapers also worked in alliances to set uniform advertising rates to minimize competition.

While instituting these cost-saving measures, newspaper leaders sought content that was most likely to be popular. Both Baldasty and Nerone identified religious publications as popular reading during the Penny Press years. Baldasty noted that religious publications lured advertisers with the promise that families who read religion periodicals were "big" consumers (1992, p. 115). Many religious periodicals took on the same function as the party press—to advocate a cause. But in the case of religious periodicals, the cause was religious, not political. Nerone (1989) characterized Americans in the nineteenth century as possessing a belief in utopias and an attraction for thinking that promoted enlightenment through the rational discussion of religious matters, and Universalist publications arguing that knowledge could progress with free inquiry.

During this period, the role of religion was still seen as a unifying principle in an otherwise changing social and cultural world. "In antebellum America the universe was sometimes mechanical and sometimes dynamic and sometimes both. But it was always divinely ordered" (Jones, 1971, p. 19). For the rank and file in the Gilded Age, Christian theology explained life, and Newtonian theory and mechanical metaphors explained society. Others, mainly intellectuals, saw a shift from the mathematical way of reasoning, from Locke to subjectivism "in which the universe did not create mind but the mind created the universe" (p. 22).

It was during this period that Herbert Spencer and others insisted that the world was improving in a kind of natural process, and the new socioeconomic theory of individualism elevated the individual as the most important ingredient in the economic mix. In this context, so the argument goes, the government should not interfere with the individual because he or she supplies the enterprise for progress. In short, this socioeconomic theory became an application of evolution in the science of economics. In this age where Christianity was still a dominant influence, new forces were gaining favor. The new journalists at times wrote reinforcing the dominant ideas and at other times challenging the order, with articles about the women's equality movement, the growth of labor, the concentration of wealth in monopolies, government corruption, and the plight of minorities. The movements shared at least one other common element, the notion of Progressivism.

Among the widespread assumptions in the nation was the belief that in evangelical Protestantism lay the possibility of redeeming society (McCormick, 1990). Driven by the middle and upper classes, this branch of Christianity possessed a sense that genuine reform in big business was possible without injuring capitalism; it also believed in the potential existence of organizations that would not injure the individual, and in government growth that would safeguard democracy. Often working as volunteers, the reformers sought public life and used the press to focus the spotlight on their work, which they considered noble and divinely mandated. Many thought that corruption, once exposed by the press, would lead righteous people to demand reform (Knowlton and Parsons, 1993, p. 179). This world was the scene of the muckrakers and it depended on the morality as expressed in Christianity for its success. The press carried reports of these crusades, in part, because of the recognition that faith with deeds made good copy. The question at this point is: What factors contributed to this reforming fervor at this point in the history of the United States? Much of it can be traced to the Social Gospel movement.

Christian Journalism and The Social Gospel

German theologians Fredrich Schleiermacher (1768-1834) and Albrecht Ritschl (1822-1889) were among the most influential theologians of their day (Shelly, 1996, p. 400; Grenz and Olsen, 1992, p. 51). Schleiermacher, in particular, revolutionized Christian thinking by shifting the emphasis from the authority of the Bible to the experience of the believer (Shelly, 1996, p. 401). He became known as the father of modern theology. Ritschl, known as the most influential theologian in the late nineteenth century and the principal teacher of American liberals, taught that "religion rests upon the values of men, not upon the truth of science" (p. 402). While Ritschl taught that a person was a product of evolution, he emphasized the value-making part of a person, a counterpoint to the biblical criticism of the day that stressed knowledge based on facts. Science could be used to establish facts, Ritschl said, but it could not rule on values.

The influence of these two theologians led to liberal theology (Shelly, 1996, p. 403). Prior to 1880, most ministers associated with the Congregationalists held to the sovereignty of God, to the innate depravity of humankind, to the atonement of Jesus Christ, to the Holy Spirit as essential to conversion, and to the eternal separation of the saved and the lost in heaven or hell. After 1880, however, Andover Seminary, established by New England Congregationalists in 1808, challenged the requirement that all faculty subscribe to the allegiance to Calvinism and the preceding tenets. By the late nineteenth century, almost every American denomination encountered a heresy of some kind (p. 404). Yet, ministers of the Gospel continued to battle the heresies because "the ministry derives its authority from the word, not vice versa" (Jenkins, 1987, p. 44).

In addition to the theological shift, the economic landscape in Europe and the United States changed drastically as factories took over cities, increasing manufacturing efficiency but adding to the despair of the people who flocked to urban centers for work (p. 406). The question of economics, particularly over the ownership of excessive amounts of property, dominated this Industrial Revolution, but the church maintained its conviction for the tenth commandment: "Thou shalt not covet thy neighbor's house ... ," suggesting that ownership was a natural and inalienable right to be enjoyed by any who could afford to do so (p. 407). In addition, the eighth commandment banning stealing was and continues to be an expectation in capitalism. Nonetheless, by the middle of the nineteenth century, many Christians worked for improved conditions for laborers by challenging the laissez faire philosophy of business and by establishing Christian institutions to relieve suffering, supporting the formation of unions, and working to pass legislation to improve working conditions (p. 409).

This interest led to a movement for social justice in the United States known as the Social Gospel, a movement which believed that God's saving work must include corporate structures committed to doing good deeds. It relied on the New Theology and progressive orthodoxy as expressed by the Andover Seminary (pp. 412-413). The most influential spokesman for the Social Gospel was Walter Rauschenbusch (1861-1918), who argued that the old message of salvation must be enlarged to include the sinfulness of every human heart and the sinfulness of the social order (pp. 413-414).

For Rauschenbusch, life on earth could evolve into the Kingdom of God as part of the evolutionary cycle. "Translate the evolutionary theories into religious faith, and you have the doctrine of the Kingdom of God. This combination with the scientific evolutionary thought has freed the kingdom ideal of its catastrophic setting and its background of demonism, and so adapted it to the climate of the modern world" (Rauschenbusch, 1912, p. 9). Rauschenbusch believed that sin slowed down the evolutionary process of the Kingdom on Earth. Specifically, sin plagued social institutions, such as the business of making capitalism evil. The concentration of wealth was contrary to the spirit of Christ and caused injustice and inequality (Ferre, 1988, p. 8).

The agenda for reform during this period was often focused in the cities (Mott, 1947, p. 194), which were home to burgeoning numbers of immigrants. In 1900, 11,562,000 or 14 percent of the nation's 81,626,000 residents were Christian, according to researcher David B. Barrett (Hutchinson, 1998, p. 50). Schudson (1978) noted that by 1900, about half the population consisted of immigrants (p. 97). These newcomers became avid readers, who used the newspaper for entertainment as much as for news. In the country, the passage of rural free delivery meant everyone, including farmers, could enjoy the ever-widening array of consumer goods presented in illustrations in the Sears catalogue (Boorstin, 1973). Boorstin called rural free delivery the most important communication revolution in American history–cheap public communication. With it came the prospect of a daily newspaper, and some farmers subscribed to up to three a day. Rural free delivery brought farmers catalogues that helped them become more like everyone else. The newspapers linked communities of the unseen, like an early version of Internet electronic bulletin boards; but these "picture books" began displacing the holy book. "The farmer kept his Bible in the frigid parlor, but as Edna Ferber remarked in *Fanny Herself*, her novel of the mail-order business, the mail-order catalogue was kept in the cozy kitchen" (Boorstin, 1973, p. 129). With the consumer culture coming within reach, newspapers lost even more of their flavor of publishing the news of the day as the work of Providence and concentrated more on the advancements that promised to save labor rather than souls.

Intent on protecting the home and family, reform-minded women organized in the late 1800s and formed single-sex associations such as church groups, literary circles, mothers' clubs, and temperance societies. "By far the largest and most important of these organizations

was the Woman's Christian Temperance Union, founded in 1874 and
bent on 'do everything' programs that included help for homeless
children, prisoners and women suffrage" (McCormick, 1990, pp. 101-
102). By the late 1890s, membership in WCTU increased but the focus
of the work narrowed to the standard of sobriety, the issue of
temperance. Furthermore, "... no other organization had ever done so
much to arouse middle class women about social problems or to draw
so many of those women in public life" (McCormick, 1990, p. 102).
The middle class, noted Jones, constituted the "bulk of newspaper
readers" who liked "cheerful religion, conventional office buildings,
upright pianos" and all things respectable (Jones, 1971, p. 183).
Newspapers wanted to appeal to these readers, not from a duty to
produce a brand of journalism that honored the divine, but to gain favor
with this burgeoning middle class.

    These members of WCTU provided a genuine alternative to the
two-party system of voting and influencing of public policy
(McCormick, 1990). McCormick noted that while WCTU and labor
groups such as the Knights of Labor and Farmers' Alliance, could not
match the political strength of Democrats and Republicans, they helped
the nation turn a corner in the practice of politics, exerting influence
from winning an office to establishing public policy. From 1893 to
1897, unemployment was staggering. It was during this period that
labor organizer Jacob S. Coxey marched with 500 tramps to
Washington, D.C., to publicize the plight of the unemployed, but armed
police intervened and pushed the men into camps. It was at this time
that ministers sought "to make Christianity relevant to the world, not
only the next, by aligning their churches actively on the side of the
disadvantaged" (McCormick, 1990, p. 104). This marked the period of
Progressivism, reform that expects government to solve problems. The
press was on hand, not to lead the crusade or advocate change, but to
chronicle the discontent as part of its mission to retain those faithful
middle-class readers. During the bleak years of industrial America,
when newspapers encouraged the nation to go to war against Spain,
rallied for the women's vote, and questioned powerful business,
Americans were casting about for moral and spiritual direction.
Religion still provided comfort, but it was under assault. Only the
tangible was real. Standardization led to measuring the world in terms
of statistics and revolutionized ways of understanding the world,
including behavior. Boorstin (1973) wrote:

        Christianity had relied on a ministry of the Gospel,
        on sacred authoritative texts, and had enlisted faith in

the authority and benevolence of a Fatherly God. But psychology, in (G. Stanley) Hall's vision, referred man to no Higher Authority (except perhaps the Psychologist). Its sacred text was experience and it made man a rule unto himself. (p. 229)

In this social climate where morality was no longer absolute but determined by each person, the need to put more muscle into recording the misdeeds of the high and mighty might be needed. Sensationalism could be explained by a drive to increase circulation or it could have been a reaction to a world ripped this way and that in the whirlwind of change on the business, educational, research, and international fronts. While the yellow news reporters perverted journalism into sensational headlines and articles, the reason that these kinds of publishers knew that readers would respond to this content was their belief that Sunday school morality was still active. Yellow journalism publishers knew their audience and the kind of behavior that would outrage it.

Newspaper publishers in the Gilded Age, like journalists of today, often concentrate undue attention on the moral failure of one of America's leaders, be it a politician, a captain of industry or a member of the clergy believing such failings to be big news. At the same time, genuine reform, such as the suffrage movement, would succeed and newspapers would help usher in the change because good news is often based on a morality that traces its roots to the ethic that says right will overcome. Moral failures and political excesses were not reported in terms of a subjective ethic of the elite, but, in terms of the world of ordinary people who, like the ancient Hebrews, looked to the Ten Commandments, as a guide for right and wrong. Yellow journalism worked because it understood that middle-class people could be outraged by the conduct of people who acted selfishly and committed acts of adultery, acts of crime and acts of betrayal.

By the nineteenth century, "news lived on after it had lost its role in religion," (Nord, 1990, p. 37). By this statement, Nord meant that news of the nineteenth century did not concentrate on the way God was at work in the community as news did in the colonial period. Instead news was redefined to be information apart from the way God may or may not be involved in the community. In the twentieth century, journalists denied that a world view colored their thinking; the objectivity that they saluted was a system where "a person's statements about the world can be trusted if they are submitted to established rules deemed legitimate by a professional community" (Schudson, 1978, p. 7). As previously quoted, Clarence Darrow wrote that in his day, 1893, "the world has grown tired of preachers and sermons; today it asks for facts. It has grown tired of fairies and angels, and asks for flesh and blood" (Schudson, 1978, p. 73).

By the end of the century, the nation was growing increasingly secular. Robert and Helen Lynn found that church and Sunday school attendance declined between 1890 and 1924 (Silk, 1995, p. 26). In addition, the amount of news coverage of religious topics in a sample market declined from 5.6% to 2.3%. A decline in news coverage of religion also was seen in a decade-by-decade study of *The New York Times* by Robert Pettit (p. 35). Kenneth Nordin also found a decline in religion news on daily and weekly newspapers that he systematically sampled for the years 1849, 1874, 1904, 1931, and 1960. Pettit's view echoed others' that the media reflect society. It was during the year 1900 that one mainstream newspaper in the Midwest reversed this trend of secularization to include Christian journalism as its dominant news. Even as early as August 19, 1836, James Gordon Bennett who made the point of the power of a newspaper in his *New York Herald* wrote (Mott, 1941, p. 232-233):

> What is to prevent a daily newspaper from being made the greatest organ of social life? Books have had their day–the theatres have had their day–the temple of religion has had its day. A newspaper can be made to take the lead of all these in the great movements of human thought and of human civilization. A newspaper can send more souls to Heaven, and save more from Hell, than all the churches or chapels in New York–besides making money at the same time. Let it be tried.

Summary

Christian journalism was practiced differently in the various periods of journalism history. In seventeenth century New England, news was linked to idea of Providence revealing His plan for the colonists. By the eighteenth century, newspapers featured content on hymns, scriptures, sermons, and the advance of the Roman Catholic Church. By the early nineteenth century, religious newspapers gained popularity; however, in the 1860s, they began to dilute their general message for all wider audiences and depended on a denominational flag-waving for survival. The general-interest Christian newspaper could not sustain an adequate paid circulation. As mainstream newspapers published fewer and fewer articles on revivals and other religious activities, Christian publishers used private printing of religious tracts with the goal in 1829 to supply a Bible to every family in the United States who needed one. In rare instances, mainstream newspapers such as the *Boston Recorder* retained a Christian identity, but by 1872, as many as 340 denominational newspapers were published in the United States. These newspapers utilized paid advertising but banned liquor and tobacco display advertisements. Newspapers such as the *Baptist Christian Register* also refused to publish patent medicine advertising. Before long, however, even these newspapers faltered.

These denominational newspapers of the nineteenth century were seen as the most promising medium to communicate the Gospel to a wide audience (Nerone, 1989, pp. 25 26). For mainstream newspaper publishers, religious content was treated as just another category of news. By 1836, Bennett established religion news coverage as a separate department in his newspaper (Buddenbaum, 1987, p. 55). Most of the mainstream newspapers covered religion and Christianity as front page news when it was an event such as Charles Finney's revival meetings as reported in Horace Greeley's *New York Tribune*. By the end of the nineteenth century, interest by editors in religion news waned, and this content was published in a section reserved for church events, syndicated features, and the International Sunday School Lesson (Delp, 1985, p. 25). The rise of scientific explanations for life, the increasingly secular nature of America, and the decline in Sunday school attendance tended to be reflected in the content of the mainstream press. Sagging readership made survival ever more difficult in the denominational press.

In the 1940s, the *North American* in Philadelphia produced a newspaper free of suggestive advertising and teeming with morality (Miller, 1987, p. 104). It failed. Two decades later in June 1960 the *New York Sun* tired its approach to publishing front-page articles on church events and by August the newspaper was revamped into a religious paper that banned ads for vices such as liquor and theater (Miller, 1987, p. 104). It returned to a secular content by late 1861. Yet another failed attempt was tried and abandoned by the *Boston Daily News* in 1869 following the scandal of a minister closely associated with the paper. He fled the country in the wake of revelation that he had committed forgery (Miller, 1987, p. 104.)

Despite these false starts and stops, suspicion that the press   could lead to reform still fired many publishers along with their faith in the Social Gospel. Christian journalism of this era that included news about Christianity was at best fashioned after Bennett's approach–religious news as another department in the newspaper.

Chapter 8

How Did The Jesus Newspaper Look?

Eisenstein found that sermons were once coupled "with news about local and foreign affairs, real estate transactions, and other mundane matters" (1995, p. 111). She went on to note that the pulpit was displaced by the periodical press, "and the dictum 'nothing sacred' came to characterize the journalist's career" (Eisenstein, 1995, p. 111). Yet in March 1900 Frederick O. Popenoe, publisher of *The Topeka Daily Capital*, handed over the pages of his daily newspaper to a preacher "to put out a newspaper edited for a week according to the standards, as nearly as possible, that Jesus Christ would probably have used" (Lo Bello, 1989, p. 2). As stated earlier, the newspaper stirred the nation and circulation soared from 11,000 to more than 360,000 for the week (Mott, 1941, p. 576). Its appeal was built on a rhetorical vision that attracted some readers and repelled most journalists.

This kind of conflict is a standard approach to analyze the development of the American press. Known generally as the Progressive approach, it views the past as "a struggle in which the liberal press was pitted on the side of freedom, liberty, democracy, and equality against the powerful forces of wealth and class" (Sloan, 1991, p. 4). Conflict raged between the rich and poor, American business and labor, and liberals and conservatives during this period. The press, however, was characterized as the defender of the downtrodden since it crusaded for social and economic reform.

This period was the milieu in which Sheldon wrote, where clergy put an emphasis on individual experience and social reform, and the press was characterized as a tool that could reshape society. The influence of Schleiermacher and Ritschl on Sheldon is evident in the editorials he wrote from March 13 to March 17, 1900. For instance, in the March 16 editorial, Sheldon wrote, "There is a better day coming. The dawn of it is seen in the moral issue that we are beginning to know are (sic) moral" (Sheldon, 1900f, p. 2). Sheldon even referred to himself as a Christian socialist who possessed a firm commitment to the U.S. Constitution (Woodworth, 1983, p. 149). In a series of six editorials, Sheldon laid out a plan of improvement for his readers using Social Gospel ideas that emphasized civic improvement through widespread individual improvement. Although he urged salvation by confession of faith in his March 14, 1900 editorial, the motivation for the conversion was to create a better world, to hasten Heaven on Earth. In the pages ahead, Sheldon's editorials are reviewed to explore his view of the world and his strategy to reform it using the pulpit of a daily newspaper's editorial. His view are explained as part of a vision that he and his readers shared.

Reaction Before the Experiment

On January 23, 1900 *The Topeka Daily Capital* devoted the entire front page and part of page 2 to announcing the experiment. The page included an inch-high bold headline in all capitals that read, "Rev. Charles M. Sheldon to edit the *Capital*." The page included a line drawing of Sheldon at the top center of the page and a line drawing of Bishop John H. Vincent at the bottom of the page. Vincent wrote a tribute to Sheldon, calling him a "Christian socialist" and a "practical idealist," echoing sentiment of Social Gospel theology. On the far left of the page under the fold, the newspaper explained some of the background of the experiment. It said that Sheldon issued a challenge to a crowd of Christian workers gathered in Detroit in July 1989. He asked, "In this day, when philanthropy munificently endows our institutions of learning, is there here a man who, recognizing the potency of the public press to make or mar our civilization, will contribute a million dollars to establish a daily Christian newspaper?" ("Unique idea," 1900, p. 1). The article went on to say that the press is a powerful institution that "convenes law-making bodies, marshals armies, builds navies. It declares wars and dictates the terms of peace. It is the die in which opinion is cast. It is the force which makes opinion effective" ("Unique idea," 1900, p. 1).

The article also said *The Topeka Daily Capital* would give Sheldon an opportunity to "demonstrate his idea of the needed reform in the daily press by tendering to the country an example of a Christian daily newspaper" ("Unique idea," 1900, p. 1). The article went on to say that the idea "may inject the Christianizing ethics of a higher civilization into the coming generation" ("Unique idea," 1900, p. 1). On page 2 Kansas Governor W. E. Stanley praised the experiment, saying, "Now that an opportunity has been afforded him [Sheldon] to realize his conception of a Christian newspaper, the result for good upon the work cannot be measured" ("From Governor Stanley," 1900, p. 2).

In addition to the hype and hopefulness expressed in *The Topeka Daily Capital*, the newspaper injected conflict to add to the unfolding drama. On January 25, 1900 *The Topeka Daily Capital* included comments on page one from Chicago-area clergy that questioned and criticized the experiment. *The Topeka Daily Capital* reprinted an article from the *Chicago Tribune* with comments from a variety of clergy. Many said the time for the experiment was too short for a fair test and that the press of 1900 was satisfactory ("These are skeptical," 1900, p. 1). The question repeated most often was how anyone could know what Jesus would do in editing a daily newspaper. J.E. Stone, rector of St. James Episcopal Church, wrote, "Nobody knows, not even Dr. Sheldon, what Jesus would have done in certain cases, and how Jesus would conduct a newspaper. Any answer to such a hypothetical question can be considered merely as the personal view of a person giving the answer, and has no other value" ("These are skeptical," 1900, p. 1).

Others such as Thomas P. Hodnett, pastor of St. Malachy's Roman Catholic Church, said that he did not believe that Jesus would edit a newspaper, but "would do just as he did when here before. He would help the poor and suffering and preach the Gospel to all" ("These are skeptical," 1900, p. 1). Some clergy suggested that the press avoid sensational detail in crime coverage but not abandon it completely and at least one minister, R.A. Torrey, pastor of Chicago Avenue Independent Church, said the experiment merely "is a clever advertisement" for *The Topeka Daily Capital* ("These are skeptical," 1900, p. 1).

While Popenoe presented the experiment as a test for mainstream newspapers, his ultimate motivation was to capitalize on Sheldon's popularity to make a sudden financial windfall. Popenoe paid just 10 percent down on a $50,000 debt to purchase *The Topeka Daily Capital* from the Bank of Topeka. During the experiment, Popenoe raised the newsstand price of the newspaper and increased the advertising rate and eventually made $30,000 for the one-week of news distribution. Popenoe succeeded in getting the nation's attention. Up to 40 newspaper correspondents covered the experiment (Lo Bello, 1989, p. 52). They had plenty to report–the absence of scandals, stock market reports and anything Sheldon deemed objectionable.

The Topeka Daily Capital kept the hype high in the days preceding the experiment with a full page reprint of articles and illustrations from the January 28, 1900 *New York Journal and Advertiser* in a page on

February 6, 1900. Also on February 6, 1900, *The Topeka Daily Capital* included a box of type on page one that said the Congregational ministers of St. Louis endorsed the Sheldon edition, adding "we pledge ourselves as individuals to take the paper during the week" ("The Christian daily," 1900, p. 1). From January 23, 1900 to March 10, 1900, *The Topeka Daily Capital* published a display advertisement to sell the week of Sheldon editions for 25 cents in advance. In addition, the editorial page included a paragraph announcing the Sheldon edition and the price of 25 cents for the Tuesday, March 13 to Saturday, March 19 issues. (*The Topeka Daily Capital* did not publish a Monday edition.) On February 11, 1900, *The Topeka Daily Capital* included an entire page of reaction from newspapers across the nation both abusing and admiring the Sheldon experiment ("Press of the nation," 1900, p. 10). By March 8, 1900, *The Topeka Daily Capital* boasted on page one that it had more than 200,000 subscriptions ("Over 200,00 subscriptions," 1900, p. 1).

The Role of the Novel

The character of Edward Norman, editor of the *Raymond Daily News*, was the persona in Sheldon's *In His Steps* who most resembled Sheldon in his real-life role as editor. In the novel, however, the Rev. Maxwell was Sheldon's alter ego. Both characters possessed Sheldon's confidence that determining God's will for the selection of news was very accessible for anyone who attempted it using the "What would Jesus do?" question. As stated earlier, Norman told his managing editor not to print a sports article about a boxing match (Sheldon, 1984, p. 31). In addition, Norman altered the newspaper's advertising policy (p. 40) and stopped its Sunday publication (p. 43). While these changes hurt business, Norman found fulfillment in behaving as he thought Jesus would behave in the same situation; nonetheless, the policies hurt the newspaper's circulation and an heiress was forced to use her personal fortune to salvage the failing publication.

Missing in the decisions made by Norman and other characters are principles that guide the decision-making process. The only guidance Sheldon offered was a vague sense that once a person poses the key question, What would Jesus do?, the answer is obvious.

For instance, when Norman tried to explain his decision not to publish an article on a professional boxing match, he said, "Clark, if Christ were editor of a daily paper, do you honestly think He would print three columns and a half of a prize fight?"

"No, I don't suppose He would."

"Well, that's my only reason for shutting this account out of the *News*. I have decided not to do anything in connection with the paper for a whole year that I honestly believe Jesus would not do" (Sheldon, 1994, p. 31).

When Sheldon edited *The Topeka Daily Capital,* he also used this kind of explanation. The logic appears to rely more on a personal sense of ethics than a systematic approach. As editor, Sheldon became Edward Norman in the flesh and followed the script Norman used in the novel. He banned smoking and profanity (Sheldon, 1925, p. 124), reviewed questionable advertising (p. 121), and hired two Saturday editors to prevent work on Sunday (p. 135). He told reporters not to publish "theatrical news nor news of prize fights" ("Declines to talk," 1900, p. 5). With all these decisions, he offered no rationale, and this ambiguity helped form the rhetorical vision that made both the novel and the Sheldon edition popular.

For purposes of this research, the six editorials of Sheldon are explored with depth. These editorials are the articles that are signed by Sheldon, firmly establishing them as his own words; however, he said he would read every word of the newspaper copy during the week he was editor (Miller, 1987, p. 118). The editorials reveal the deepest sentiments of the Sheldon experiment including policy issues and rationale for the Sheldon edition. As an artifact, these editorials best represent the clearest example of Sheldon's approach to Christian journalism and are explored for the manifest and latent content. Before examining the editorials, it is helpful to review the news of The Jesus Newspaper.

The News of the Sheldon Edition

To gain a sense of the news that Sheldon published in thirty-six column news inches in each of his editions, the front pages are discussed. Sheldon's first front page on Tuesday, March 13, 1900 featured a prayer from Bishop Vincent, the same clergyman who praised Sheldon on page one of the January 23, 1900 *Topeka Daily Capital* when it announced the Sheldon experiment. The newspaper included an article with the headline, "Starving India, Fifty million people affected by the famine." The news, although weeks old, provoked Sheldon to action. Under it was a sidebar article by the Rev. H.J. Bruce with a first-person narrative about the famine and a report from Curzon, viceroy of India, on the suffering. Sheldon included an editor's note that he signed that said, "The *Capital* knows of no more important matter of news the world over this morning than the pitiable condition of famine-stricken India. We give the latest and fullest available information of the progress of the scourge in the following articles" (Sheldon, 1900i, p. 1). Sheldon's note went on to solicit a 10-cent contribution from every reader for a relief fund, but many readers contributed much more.

The front page also carried three opinion pieces denouncing war (Thomas, 1900, p. 1; Bright, 1900, p. 1). The front page featured two essays on Prohibition (Howard, 1900, p. 1; "Prohibition tested," 1900, p. 1). The final article was a letter to the editor requesting help for people with tuberculosis (Danner, 1900, p. 1).

The only traditional news article on page one was the update on an East India famine. The rest of the articles, although signed, were opinion pieces but not labeled as such. They were reprints from other periodicals. No art or illustrations appeared on page one of the first issue or the last issue, the evening of March 17, 1900. The other front pages had an illustration or, in the case of morning newspaper on March 17, 1900, the graphic element of a poem and a song lyric. Other newspapers that day reported the bubonic plague in San Francisco, a tenement fire in Newark, New Jersey, the wounding of eight American soldiers in the Philippines and the death of the Italian boxer Guydo, who died as the result of a blow struck by James J. Jeffries in a boxing match (Ripley, 1965, pp. 22-23). These news stories did not make *The Topeka Daily Capital.* For many critics, the publishing of a death from a sporting event could have supported Sheldon's conviction that boxing is violent and add power to the clergyman's idea that boxing is deadly and unworthy fare for a uplifting periodical.

On Wednesday, March 14, 1900, *The Topeka Daily Capital* led with an article by editor H.T. Chase on the response to Sheldon's Tuesday appeal for famine relief (p. 1). Chase said readers could send donations to the *Christian Endeavor World* of Boston as well as other church organizations. Beside this article was a four-column illustration denouncing war. Below it was an article without a headline that listed the latest casualties by name from in the war in the Philippines ("For the sake of humanity," 1900, p. 1).

Sheldon ran two letters to the editor on page one. The first was from Wilbur F. Crafts, superintendent of the Reform Bureau, on the encroachment of business on Sunday (1900, p. 1). The other was from Kansas Governor W.E. Stanley, who wrote about prison reform that he initiated and its benefits (1900, p. 1). Next to the Crafts's letter was an article that outlined the cost of crime to taxpayers. At the conclusion of the article was a note from Sheldon in brackets that moralized about the cost of crime, saying that punishing crime is more expensive than preventing crime. He wrote, "As soon as humanity begins to spend more in saving its children and less on punishing them after they have begun to be lost, so soon society will inevitably reduce the cost of crime by reducing crime" (Sheldon, 1900b, p. 1).

In the center of the front page was an article on New Zealand's attempt to create a society where no one is either rich or poor. Next to it was nearly two columns of text on the progress of a socialist movement.

The front page also included fillers on the amount of grain in Kansas, the date the Paris exhibition would be held, April 15, construction of cable from Washington state to Alaska, and a request to county commissioners to elect a delegate for an upcoming conference on charities.

Sheldon also penned a piece on "The Union of Christendom" where he encouraged denominations to unite for the Prohibition cause and to uphold Sunday as a day of rest and worship. He used the idea of "one common Master" to rally Christians to love others and "win the world to faith in the Savior and to life everlasting" (Sheldon, 1900m, p. 1).

An article with the headline "They Teach Suicide" was a reprint of a pamphlet alleging that a fraternity known as the Bohemian Fraternal Benefit society encourages its members to practice infidelity, and this sin leads to suicide. This article covered three columns. A brief article by Sheldon, "Use of tobacco," described the dangers of tobacco among boys, including a sense of nervousness. Sheldon interjected his opinion in the report, asking, "But isn't it fair to ask the question, how soon will a boy be likely to stop using tobacco as long as the man who employs him is constantly using it? The responsibility in this matter rests with the grown up people. The use of tobacco is a habit that a man ought not to have for the sake of the boy who ought not to have it" (Sheldon, 1900o, p. 1).

An article on "Mormonism at Home" said that the Mormon faith was not spreading. J.W. Gleed wrote an article on a tax on alcohol. Another article discussed a Switzerland model of vote distribution ("A fair suffrage," 1900n, 1).

Another three-column illustrated dominated the Friday, March 16, 1900 issue; this one denounced war. The article that accompanied it took a pacifist view and began with an editor's note from Sheldon that said, "Christian civilization is a misnomer if its accompanying effects are seen in the exercise of brute force. It is not Christian civilization; it is barbarism" (Sheldon, 1900a, p. 1).

Another editor's note accompanied an article on a kind of domestic Peace Corps called the Social Settlement Movement. Sheldon endorsed the approach, saying, "One side of the Atonement is summed up in the words spoken of Christ–"He gave Himself." The Social Settlement Movement represents personal hand-to-hand work with men and for men. It is of enough importance to engage the prayers, the gifts and the attention of a whole world," (Sheldon, 1900h, p. 1).

Other articles discussed Standard Oil's dividends to investors and described in detail the benefits of privatizing utilities. This edition also carried two follow-up articles on famine relief.

A poem titled "If Christ should come today" and the lyrics and score of "A morning prayer" were featured on the front page Saturday morning, March 17, 1900. A note that was boxed urged readers to remember the Sabbath day and keep it holy. Following this brief was a series of articles that discussed working on Sunday.

Sheldon wrote about the newspaper's advertising policy that said patent medicine advertising was banned because Sheldon did not have time to investigate the claims of each product. He apologized for printing, by mistake, a display advertisement that appeared March 16 for a plow that used references to Christ with the sales pitch. On March 21, 1900, *The New York Tribune* lampooned Sheldon for the advertisement that said the plow stirs the subsoil deep and it was able to let in the rains that refresh the earth. "Otherwise, a large portion of moisture graciously sent by our Heavenly Father is wasted by running from the surface," the advertisement said. It went on to say that the plow manufacturer believed that it produced the kind of digger that Jesus would approved because He would not want anything to go to waste (p. 3). Sheldon also told his readers on Saturday morning that the newspaper had published an advertisement on a cream separator, but he had not had time to examine the separator to evaluate its merits (Miller, 1987, p. 121).

Sheldon urged readers to support their newspaper with "good clean advertising" to block the temptation to accept questionable advertising including liquor advertisements (Sheldon, 1900g, p. 1).

Earlier in the week, editor John Dougall wrote a history of his Christian newspaper on page 1. In it, he lobbied for the establishment of Christian newspapers. Sheldon also wrote about the feasibility of a Christian daily newspaper and invited readers to send their ideas to the newspaper then he wrote, "I shall never be connected with this or any other newspaper as editor or manager in any way whatever. My work lies along entirely different lines in my parish and my platform work" (Sheldon, 1900e, p. 1).

Beneath this article was a collection of definitions of news by various journalists. A.C. Babize, the *sub rosa* press agent for *The Topeka Daily Capital* and reporter for the *Chicago Times-Herald*, defined news as "the latest happenings anywhere in the world" ("What is news," 1900, p. 1). John H. Raftery of the *Chicago Record* said news was "a truthful statement of the latest important and interesting happenings in the world, given without coloring and with a view to the wants of the reading public" ("What is news?," 1900, p. 1).

The newspaper carried articles on the benefits of an uniform Sunday school lesson and suggested ways to make a funeral conform to good taste while retaining a Christian influence. Sheldon added an editor's note to this article that endorsed the idea of a private funeral with friends. He said Christians should seek reform in funerals to eliminate the public displays such as funeral trains (Sheldon, 1900d, p. 1).

The last front page in the series on Saturday evening, March 17, 1900, carried an article on "The Bible: The Basis of our Civilization." Sheldon printed the Sermon on the Mount, and reprinted scripture on usury, the Sabbath, money, and riches. The rest of the newspaper contained similar articles. No illustrations appeared on page one.

For Sheldon, the news pages were a warm-up for the main event of moralizing about the issues of personal and community reform featured in the six editorials. Sheldon used his front pages to highlight personal reform such as temperance and vague ideas of love and selflessness. His news articles, that read more like opinion pieces, urged social reform such a ban on war, non-partisan politics and capitalism without greed.

Sheldon used his other front-page articles to describe his approach to his ideal Christian daily newspaper where organizational policies were consistent with the values of 1900. For instance, he urged newspapers to seek reform by accepting display advertising that was circumspect, a reform in the business side of the operation. He also asked readers to practice reader reform by supporting community newspapers with advertising that was not questionable to remove the temptation from publishers to accept other lucrative but questionable advertising just to stay in business. Sheldon's other newspaper reform crossed over from journalist to reader with his ban on Sunday work and Sunday pleasures, a ban on illicit use of time. The Sunday issue also revealed Sheldon's interest in the Ten Commandments as a foundational set of rules to govern all behavior. The articles on famine relief spotlighted news in the traditional news but bent the issue as an opportunity to act on Christian principles of helping a neighbor in distress.

The idea of news to prompt action was common during Sheldon's day of crusading newspapers. That tradition remains in twenty-first century journalism. Today the practice is known as reader services where articles include contacts where readers can respond. Sheldon's twist was featuring commentary next to the news report, although Sheldon's news contained strident opinions making it more commentary than detached reporting. The news section was designed to reveal Sheldon's list of pet issues, either by the writer interjecting blatant views such as condemnation of alcohol or by the virtue of the selection of the article such as a list of soldiers who died in the war in the Philippines. In each issue, Sheldon self-consciously set the agenda by loading his front page with articles associated with the issues with which he sought reform.

The eight-pages of the broadsheet publication limited Sheldon in his variety of news, but he attempted to make every article contain a position. For Sheldon, the concept of a Christian daily newspaper was bound up in excessive, relentless commentary that insisted that a reader take a prescribed view on a topic. While the Jesus question allowed wide liberty in answers, Sheldon's commentary allowed no liberty in disagreements. Sheldon presented his views as exclusive and sanctioned by scripture and the divine. To disagree would be to challenge Providence. Sheldon's vague ideas that a person was a Christian by virtue of his love and selflessness also suggested that the same person was not a Christian if he did not possess the same opinion on Sheldon's list of reform.

Throughout, Sheldon's vision of the world runs a contradictory approach. The Jesus question allows personal answers but Sheldon's views on issues amounted to directives not to be disobeyed. To be a Christian amounts to identifying with a prescriptive Christian position, an idea that is counter to all the variety found in Christian theology and practice. The process to become a member of the church is vague and not addressed in specifics in The Jesus Newspaper. The classical evangelical position is based on Martin Luther's idea that salvation is through grace by faith alone in the sacrificial work of God's son. Sheldon presented this Gospel, but may have confused some readers with what could be interpreted as additional demands that are required to make a person a Christian. Luther pointed to the Book of James and urged salvation by faith alone without human works; Sheldon would no doubt agree, but his readers may have thought that orthodoxy required accepting Sheldon's views on Prohibition, wealth-redistribution, and all the other issues raised by The Jesus Newspaper.

Sheldon told readers in his news pages and his editorials to seek the Kingdom of God, but he does not give any strategy about this action except to endorse his views on the reform issues. In a sense, Sheldon argued for a kind of easy believism where a person could consider himself a Christian if he shared Sheldon's view on the issues he highlighted in his week of editorials. Some of the reform Sheldon endorsed was so vague as to include anyone. He told readers to love and act selflessly. In short, gaining the identity of a Christian did not require much from a person; however, retaining that identity demanded adherence to Sheldon's views on his reform issues. To be a believer after Sheldon's prescription required a person to agree to personal reform, which included vague ideas about repenting and being born again, and community reform that included Prohibition and a ban on Sunday work. While not as dogmatic, Sheldon also insisted on pacifism and income reform to eliminate pooling of vast wealth. Sheldon's world was both easy and Draconian at the same time, creating a unique blend of no demands and excessive demands.

Spiritual Interrogation and Sheldon's Editorials

Sheldon presented his rhetorical   vision in increments and always used lists to make his case. Borrowing from the respect for science's adherence to a logical development of ideas, Sheldon explained his definitions, first for an ideal newspaper, the Christian daily (March 13), then for the ideal person (March 14), then for the ideal world (March 15). He then zeroed in on the two problems of the age, alcohol and social problems that prevented the ideal world from appearing (March 16 and 17) and condemned the one problem that the press created that contributed to the loss of the ideal world–Sunday publication (March 17).

To understand Sheldon's rhetorical vision in a more detailed explanation, the full text of each of the six editorials appear in the Appendix. As stated earlier, the Sheldon editorials were published from March 13, 1900 through March 17, 1900, always in the left-side of the page 2, labeled Editorial Page, except for the editorial in the evening edition Saturday, March 17. That editorial appeared on the top, right-hand side of page one. This position, sometimes called the lead position, is reserved for the most important news of the day.

The Ideal Christian Daily Newspaper

The editorials were composed of points, sometimes numbered and other times not. For instance, Tuesday's editorial, the first of the series, outlined Sheldon's approach to newspapering and noted in sketchy detail the invitation to edit the newspaper "as a distinctly Christian daily" (Sheldon, 1900l, p. 2). He wrote, "The only thing I or any other Christian man can do in the interpretation of what is Christian in the conduct of this paper is to define the term Christian the best that can be done after asking for divine wisdom, and not judge others who might with equal desire and sincerity interpret the probable action of Jesus in a different manner" (p. 2).

Again, the Spiritual Interrogation vision did not mandate an absolute answer, but relied on personal revealed truth. Drawing on the liberal theology of Schleiermacher, Sheldon based his approach on the same kind of human experience that Schleiermacher used for his theology (Grenz and Olsen, 1992, p. 43). Both men said knowledge could be known through intuition. Schleiermacher argued that people participated in an experience rather than a timeless, authoritative system. Like Schleiermacher, Sheldon waived a claim to science and relied on insight as *sui generis*, " . . . something human in its own right and of its own kind . . ." (Grenz and Olson, 1992, p. 45).

Sheldon's first editorial in the sequence went on to list nine qualities of his operating policy:

1. He defined news as anything in the way of daily events that might contribute to a life of righteousness.

2. The newspaper would be nonpartisan.

3. The newspaper would advocate the eradication of the liquor trade.

4. Social issues such as greed, "commercially or politically, will be considered as of more serious consequence to us as a people than many other matters which too often engage the time and attention of mankind" (Sheldon, 1900l, p. 2).

5. War would be denounced.

6. On matters where the editor has no fixed opinion, the matter would not be presented as dogmatic.

7. The mission of the newspaper would be to influence readers to seek the Kingdom of God.

8. Significant reports would be signed (given bylines).

9. The Sunday paper would be published Saturday evening.

Respected journalism professor Melvin Mencher (1999) described news as possessing at least six qualities; news has importance, it speaks of the unusual, it is about people of prominence, it refers to conflict, it concerns events close to a reader's home, and it is timely (p. 134). Sheldon's definition treats news from a more cosmic view, where news content could have an eternal impact demanding much from the reader. Readers were expected to actively engage the content and treat the information as authoritative as a person might read a list of survival tips.

The list as a device in Sheldon's editorials harkens back to the model list of the Ten Commandments. Also know as the Decalogue, the Ten Commandments were given by God to Moses on Mount Sinai as recorded in Exodus and Deuteronomy in the Old Testament. The commandments deal with a person's relationship to God and a person's relationship to others. The commandments prohibit:

1. Worship of any other deity but God.

2. Worshipping idols.

3. Using God's name in vain.

In addition, the commandments call for

4. Observing the Sabbath.

5. Honoring parents.

  6. Prohibition of murder.
  7. Prohibition of adultery.
  8. Prohibition of stealing.
  9. Prohibition of giving false testimony, and
  10. Prohibition of coveting of property.

In his Saturday evening editorial, Sheldon cited one of the fourth commandments regarding not working on Sunday. He wrote seven paragraphs that highlighted the benefits of avoiding work on Sunday. The Ten Commandments were such a part of his identity that Sheldon used the work-prohibition commandment to complete his Spiritual Interrogation vision. A ban on Sunday newspapers was not unthinkable. The Presbyterian denomination went to court to prevent the publication of Sunday newspapers in Pittsburgh in 1893 using Pennsylvania blue laws that restricted commerce on Sunday (Mott, 1941, p. 584).

For Sheldon, however, the use of this commandment as his parting editorial reinforced his heroic character in the drama, making him a kind of Christ figure. By emphasizing the return to Sunday as a holy day, Sheldon established his position as absolute. Anyone who disagreed with him, disagreed with the Bible. This position is a break from the Jesus-question approach where answers are personal and not necessarily the same for everyone. The Spiritual Interrogation vision relied on the authority of scripture. This reverence for the Ten Commandments was the only part of the Spiritual Interrogation vision that must be accepted by all who asked the Jesus question.

The Ten Commandments concerned a person's obligation to others and a person's responsibility to God but they provide little rationale for the banned behavior or the proscribed behavior. Obedience is demanded because the commands are divine and not to be questioned. The Bible says obedience will be rewarded and disobedience will be punished. Sheldon's lists resembled this kind of contract where different personal and organizational responsibilities were outlined along with the penalties for violating the contract or the benefits for obeying the contract. He, too, wrote as the authority, calling some behavior such as an association with alcohol sinful. The matter was black and white, without any qualification. In these cases, Sheldon did not cite biblical proofs for the offending behavior, but just called them sin. The rationale black-out was in keeping with Sheldon's rhetorical vision where once a person posed the Jesus question, the answer he or she adopted was correct. In proactive behavior such as donating wealth to a good cause as Rachel Winslow did in *In His Steps*, the answers might vary from person to person; however, in matters of behavior to be avoided, the Jesus question would provide consistency to all who asked.

On Tuesday when Sheldon outlined his plan for a newspaper that could be edited using Christian ideology, Sheldon used the personal pronoun "I" frequently. He wrote, "I have accepted the invitation" to edit the newspaper (p. 2) and "With the hearty co-operation (sic) of every man connected with the paper and with the help of the wisdom that I have prayed might be given me from Him who is wiser than any of us, I shall do the best I can." He continued, "The only thing I or any other Christian man can do in the interpretation of what is Christian in the conduct of this paper is to define the term Christian the best that can be done after asking for divine wisdom, and not judge others who might with equal desire and sincerity interpret the probable action of Jesus in a different manner. With this understanding of the conduct of the paper this week, I will state in part its general purpose and policy."

The frequent use of the pronoun "I" established Sheldon as the authority. The use of the pronoun suggested Sheldon's responsibility to the idealized newspaper culture. In one sense, it was his responsibility to an organization and institution, but in another sense, it was his responsibility to his readers, people he thought shared his Spiritual Interrogation. It was a person-to-person relationship. The editorial opened with a general statement that defined news in item one of the list and detailed specific applications of the "news-as-developing-righteousness," including non-partisanship (item 2) and favoring Prohibition (item 3). The next general statement concerned commentary on social issues (item 4) and offered two specific examples, abhorrence of war (item 6) and open-endedness on other matters such as finances (item 6).

In item 7, however, Sheldon wrote, "The main purpose of the paper will be to influence its readers to seek first the Kingdom of God. A nation seeking the Kingdom of God, first of all, will in time find right answers to all disputed questions and become a powerful and useful nation" (p. 2). This general statement, coming as it did near the end of the nine-item list, was a fulcrum that mimics the structure of the Ten Commandments where the imperatives are divided between a person's obligation to others and a person's role to God. Item 8 noted that all articles written by reporters would be signed. This imperative suggested that the role of the reporter, a person, was altruistic. The reporter was committed to his audience, to others. As a contract, it suggests that the labor of the writer would be recognized by the byline, allowing the writer to gain a sense of satisfaction that readers would know the writer penned the article. In addition, the byline made the writer accountable to the readers. Following the pattern in scripture, the idea was that a person who obeyed (writes factually) will find earthly and heavenly rewards, but a person who disobeyed (reports in error) will find hardship.

Item 9 said *The Topeka Daily Capital* would not publish a Sunday newspaper but would substitute an evening Saturday newspaper. This specific action would appear to be better placed in the earlier list of specifics, but by its placement at the end of the lists, it followed the mandate of item 7 of the mission of pointing readers to God. The Sunday-newspaper ban demonstrated the idea of a person's role to God. In item 8, Sheldon stated his policy of recognizing achievement inside the newspaper's organization by mandating bylines; in item 9, Sheldon recognized God's role in society by mandating conduct outside the newspaper by banning Sunday publishing. The hierarchical arrangement varied from general statements to specific examples. In this way, Sheldon demonstrated the idea that each Christian was responsible for his part of the vineyard, not someone else's. If a Christian editor could ban a Sunday product and his conscience told him to do so, he was being obedient to God. However, that same person who had no control over the policy governing or over other institutions was not held accountable. A person's role and responsibility to others was restricted by his circumstances.

Accountability based on a person's role to himself or herself, a person's role to others and a person's role to God dominated Sheldon's editorials. By using this kind of approach, Sheldon established himself as the authority figure with access to insight others may not possess, particularly if they have not asked the Jesus question. The Spiritual Interrogation vision allowed too much flexibility in making decisions, so Sheldon had to position himself as more in touch with spiritual insight to demonstrate how the ideal Christian daily would appear. In Sheldon's editorials, the lists lent themselves to this framework and blended well with the overall break from standard newspaper convention. Most newspaper editorials then as now advocate reform from public-policy change while Sheldon advocated reform from personal change. By establishing himself as the authority, Sheldon could be above the convention of the usual give-and-take decision-making in public policy matters and just issue fiats. Although the Jesus question produces personal answers, the answer carried with it the authority of the divine and debate was unnecessary.

The Ideal Person, Community and World

The ideas of hierarchy and responsibility continued in the ordering of the editorials. While the first editorial on March 13, 1900 started with Sheldon's personal responsibility and the order that he intended to impose on his newsroom, the second editorial on March 14, 1900 focused on people and their responsibilities. Here the pronoun "we" is used frequently. Sheldon included himself in this list that examined the qualities of "better men and women" (p. 2). The third editorial on March 15, 1900 expanded the vision to the world. The progression proceeded from one person (Sheldon on Tuesday) to others in the community (Sheldon and the residents of Topeka on Wednesday) to the world ("The World's Greatest Need" on Thursday). On March 16, 1900, Thursday, Sheldon wrote of moral issues and suggested the contractual penalty for disobedience, loss of salvation and the persistence of selfishness. In the morning March 17, 1900 editorial, Sheldon wrote of an example of a sin that has gone unchallenged, the use of alcohol, and argued in four open letters for its banishment as a way to use personal reform to enact public policy reform.

Like an Old Testament prophet, Sheldon assumed the role of a patriarch who adopted the oratory of preaching to the written text. As a narrative device, he used the list but the style is that of a sermon with imperatives that often end in prayer on some level. The function of the imperatives is to shut off debate by giving the items the power of commands. By listing the solution to personal and public reform as commands, Sheldon drew on the Social Gospel theology of the day, which held experience as key and social action as its manifestation. Writing as he does during the Progressive period, Sheldon implied by virtue of printing his editorials that the press can make a difference in personal and public reform. The contract idea suggested that once the ideas are disseminated, individuals would be reformed with uniform results. Informing this approach was Sheldon's clergy background that used directives to accomplish the task. The idea was that readers should respond because God said obey. As a minister, Sheldon spoke for God and presented positions that allowed little room to challenge the message. These editorials use the technique of defamilization by drawing readers away from the rational discourse of the conventional editorial to Sheldon's approach of the directive. In this way, his editorials are not the standard commentary written by an editor with the support of a newspaper. Instead, Sheldon is writing in the tradition of the Old Testament prophets who speak with divine authority as mouthpieces of God.

Sheldon as a Writer of an Epistle

Another way of looking at Sheldon's work is as an letter, called an epistle in the New Testament. Sheldon approached his editorials as if he were a New Testament writer penning an epistle to a church. Much is assumed by Sheldon of his readers including reverence for the fundamentals of the faith as outlined in the Niagara Conference of 1876: the verbal and inerrant inspiration of the Bible, the virgin birth, substitutionary atonement, bodily resurrection, and the imminent second coming of Jesus Christ (Ferre, 1988, p. 5). His references to deity, sin, the Kingdom of God, and other biblical allusions suggest Sheldon considered his readers to be well acquainted with the language of orthodox Christianity. For instance, in his six editorials, Sheldon referred to sin, sins, or sinner a total of 17 times and to the Kingdom of God five times.

Sheldon's six editorials from March 13 to March 17, 1900 can be read as if they were six chapters in a New Testament book. Overall, the theme of the book was that a Christian daily newspaper was possible and it could be used to usher in Heaven on Earth. How? Through reform. Sheldon used the strategy of the best behavior modification techniques where improper behavior is replaced with proper behavior. Borrowing an idea from Colossians, readers were told to put off sinful behavior and put on godly behavior. The idea is that behavior is like a garment that can be shed and replaced with a new garment.

Sheldon used this put off/put on approach in all of his editorials to suggest reform, a popular theme in business, government and community work in 1900. Sheldon called for reform in the press, the first and last editorials, reform of the community, reform of individual's responses to admonitions, reform of the government, reform of liquor use and reform of the use of time on Sunday.

The first and last editorials that highlight press reform emphasized Sheldon's goal to model a Christian daily newspaper for the week to demonstrate the kind of content the newspaper should contain along with specifics concerning policies. For instance, the first editorial on March 13, 1900 listed nine features of the ideal Christian daily newspaper, features his Sheldon edition possessed.

They were:

1. The Sheldon edition would be a newspaper.
2. The Sheldon edition would be non-partisan.
3. The Sheldon edition would be pro-prohibition.
4. The Sheldon edition would highlight social problems particularly selfishness and greed.
5. The Sheldon edition would be anti-war.
6. The Sheldon edition would be neutral on issues that were not matters of character such as finances.
7. The Sheldon edition's main goal would be to influence readers to see the Kingdom of God so that they can find answers and improve the nation.
8. The Sheldon edition would have signed editorials and news articles.

9. The Sheldon edition would not have a Sunday edition but two Saturday editions.

The last editorial on Saturday evening, March 17, 1900, read like a kind of a formal deductive syllogism known as an enthymeme, a popular rhetorical device where the audience helps construct the proof (Griffin, 1997, p. 305).

In an ordinary syllogism, a major premise is followed by a minor premise that leads to a conclusion.

Major premise: All people are created equal.

Minor premise: I am a person.

Conclusion: I am equal to other people.

In the enthymeme, the minor premise or conclusion must be provided by the audience. In Sheldon's last editorial, he wrote:

Major premise: Obedience to God means no working on Sunday.

Minor premise: This Saturday night edition for Sunday reading was produced without any work on Sunday.

The missing element, the conclusion, is that Sheldon was obedient to God by producing a newspaper that did not require any work on a holy day.

This editorial suggested the general premises that no work should be accomplished on Sunday and everyone should be obedient to God.

The two editorials combined suggested dramatic press reform. Sheldon argued that a daily Christian newspaper must have specific characteristics such as an anti-liquor policy, but he generalized that all general-circulation newspapers that want to be obedient to God must have the same characteristics.

In his second editorial, March 14, 1900, Sheldon called for community reform where individuals were told to put off selfishness and put on regeneration. Sheldon's weakness in all his editorials was that his directions on implementing the reform was very vague. The exceptions are the editorials that are specific to the issues of liquor use and Sunday work. In all but these two editorials, Sheldon called for personal regeneration but neglected to explain how a reader could gain regeneration.

In the third editorial, Sheldon called for response reform. He wrote that when someone proposed a plan to improve something, a reference to Sheldon's experiment to reform the daily press, others are critical of the idea. Sheldon called for putting off criticism and putting on unity. He also urged a non-partisan approach to government. Again, his admonitions lacked specifics. The readers had to fill in these missing steps.

The fourth editorial, March 16, 1900, called for government reform and Sheldon argued exclusively to cease behavior that supported liquor or inequities in business. He told his readers to stop supporting liquor trade. Using the familiar scriptural idea of putting off and putting on, Sheldon urged reform. He urged putting off unfair practices where the wealthy get wealthier and capitalists profited unduly. Readers, again, were expected to provide their own approach on fulfilling this reform.

The fifth editorial discussed the use of liquor and demanded that anyone connected with liquor at all to put off that behavior. Sheldon specifically called for the putting off of manufacturing of liquor, the putting off of political support for liquor, the putting off of the private use of liquor and the putting on of consistent law enforcement. Sheldon does not explain how a railroad employee was to stop his association with his employer if the coach served liquor in the dining cars. Short of quitting, a solution was left up to the reader.

For Sheldon, his week of editorials relied heavily on readers to provide the missing solution on specific ways to make these reform policies work. Sheldon could be praised for demanding so much from his audience that he would leave the missing premise or conclusion to each reader's imagination; however, what is more likely is that Sheldon could not suggest practical ways to make his elaborate reforms become a reality.

Nonetheless, the world that could be achieved with Sheldon's reform was meant to be an attractive incentive. His world would be filled with people who did not drink, who were not selfish, who did not act with a partisan spirit, who did not criticize, and who honored Sunday as a day of worship. This world of "not" behavior, where everyone avoided certain behavior, was made possible by adherence to a new holy document, the Christian daily newspaper, which constantly reminded readers that they must not do certain acts, but it was up to them to figure out how to implement the changes.

This regimented world was Sheldon's view of Heaven on Earth; for others it may have sounded like a restricted society where deviations from the prescribed behavior could lead to consequences. Sheldon's world left little room for unconventional thinking. Its directive approach was counter to the tradition and history of American journalism where democracy meant giving voice to opinions that deviate from the majority.

Sheldon's world did not allow for much deviation and the kind of press he proposed was crippled by the very feature that makes Christianity so vibrant: liberty of expression. All of history is testament that God created humankind to freely worship Him. The vast number of denominations prove that yielded men and women approach worship with vastly different expectations. The Sheldon approach prescribed a legalistic approach to Christianity, where works, rather than faith, marked a person as a believer. The Sheldon edition promoted a kind of journalism that emphasized the appearance of righteousness that was one-dimensional and too simplistic to challenge many to consider the claims of a Creator.

Use of Repetitive Language

Another organizing device that Sheldon used during his week as editor was repetition. On March 13, Sheldon had six references to deity, three references to good behavior and two references to activities to avoid. On March 14, he had three references to deity and 15 to good conduct. On March 15, Sheldon had 13 references to deity, seven to good conduct, and one to activities to avoid. On March 16, he had two references to deity, three to good conduct, and six to activities to avoid. In the March 17 morning editorial, he has 11 to deity and three to activities to avoid. In the final editorial, Sheldon had nine references to deity, three to good behavior and one to activities to avoid. The first and last editorials provide some sense of closure by using "Christian" as an adjective. The March 13 editorial used Christian as an adjective 10 times and the last editorial used Christian as an adjective three times.

Sheldon invoked references to deity to align himself as the spiritual authority who could speak for the divine, part of his role as shepherd to his expanded congregation of readers. The references to deity also support his mandates against sins such as selfishness and greed. Sheldon called for good behavior and denounced activities to avoid using the language of the pulpit. He talked of righteousness and evil and sin in general but spoke of only one specific evil in four editorials.

The greatest sin of the age for Sheldon was liquor. Shortly before his death, Sheldon told a writer what he thought Jesus would do and listed battling alcohol as one of three missions (Ferre, 1988, p. 42). The other two tasks were promoting Christian unity against war and social differences and preserving the family.

Liquor or temperance was mentioned in Sheldon's editorials Tuesday, Wednesday, Friday and Saturday. Part of the organizational strategy for Sheldon's work was to highlight a person's responsibility to himself or herself. Alcohol use and the way it could influence a person's behavior was an example that allowed Sheldon to cross over from the responsibility a person had to himself to his role with others. By making a personal change in a person's role to himself, the change would impact his role with others.

For instance, Wednesday's editorial was a six-item list that used Sheldon's general-statement-to-specific-example approach to suggest a person's responsibility to God and a person's responsibility to himself or herself. The headline for the editorial is "Better men and women" (p. 2) and concerned ways to make Topeka a better city. The editorial began with imperatives to tell the truth, keep pure, act unselfishly and love one another (item one). This first item could be the beatitudes compressed into a paragraph. Sheldon quoted Scripture to support the idea. Here Sheldon is borrowing from homiletics (preaching) where Scripture is used for applications (Hastings, 1919, p. 215). His preaching editorials suggested the kind of creator of a media artifact that Bordwell (1989, p. 45) described when a film director projects his personality onto the work. As author of the editorials, Sheldon not only projected a preaching style, but a strong-willed personality brimming with clarity of conviction to the point of rigidity. The lists also reflected a simplicity in Sheldon's rhetoric in addition to a simplicity in life and deed. He allowed no drinking, a clear imperative, rather than an occasional drink for celebrations or special occasions. This stark black-white world where war is denounced without qualification added to the fantasy of an uncomplicated approach to life's hard questions. By definition, evangelical Christians would support the simple idea of salvation or damnation, but many, then as today, would be less deliberate on "either-or" matters of alcohol consumption or the necessity of military action.

In Wednesday's editorial, Sheldon issued his imperatives that call for a personal response (items 1-5). The list of imperatives on personal conduct were characteristics of living the Christian life and included telling the truth, doing God's will, acting non-partisan in government and avoiding criticism without knowing the facts. All these imperatives were presented as the fruit of a Christian spirit once a person has followed item 7 from the first day's editorial about salvation, a personal policy issue. Implied in a person's salvation was asking the Jesus question. The last item in Wednesday's editorial concerned Topeka's 65 denominations acting together for the temperance movement, where Sheldon made a public policy plea. This plea was consistent with his person's-responsibility-to-God approach.

When salvation was highlighted as it was in Thursday, March 15, 1900 editorial, Sheldon did not end in a blatant prayer. The Spiritual Interrogation vision was sensitive to people who have not asked the Jesus question and who can not be expected to be enlightened. For these people, the best that can be done is to persuade them to join the participants in the rhetorical vision using an implied prayer.

In the third editorial, Thursday, Sheldon wrote of "The world's greatest need" (1900r, p. 2). He used the language of prayer in his prose writing, "Ye must be born again" and "Seek ye first the Kingdom of God" (Sheldon, 1900s, p. 2). The lack of a prayer in an otherwise personal salvation appeal kept within the contractual framework where Sheldon treated the responsibility of a person's role to God, not as a personal issue, but as a group issue. In discussing the world, he referred to "them," the broadest possible group, and suggested that salvation of souls would be good public policy. "Selfishness is at the bottom of the world's trouble," Sheldon (1900s, p. 2) wrote and recalled the idea of the Social Gospel where organizations had a responsibility to overcome the fallen nature of their enterprise to eliminate suffering caused by selfishness. The contractual promise occurred here: "And as fast as it is taken away by the power of Christ, as He is allowed to come into the daily life, so fast will the life of men on the earth become the happy, strong, beautiful life that God longs to have it" (Sheldon, 1900s, p. 2).

While Sheldon interjected scripture and "preaching" throughout his editorials, the prayer worked as another device in the contractual schematic. The first editorial Tuesday ended with a prayer: "May God bless the use of this paper to the glory of His Kingdom on earth" (Sheldon, 1900l, p. 2). The thrust of the first editorial was Sheldon's personal response to the job of editing. While Wednesday's editorial included personal responsibility imperatives in items 1-5, it ended with a call for churches to do "our share." This editorial did not end in prayer, a kind of recognition that to be effective, prayer must be part of personal piety. Prayer was for the believer according to the biblical contract that indicated God responds only to those who have a relationship with Him, or want to seek a relationship with Him. The contract in the editorial assumed that in prayer, a person talking to God, was a personal policy issue but was inappropriate when working at the organizational level, particularly government.

Sheldon operated on the idea of responsibility and branched from a person's role to himself or herself to a person's role to others to a person's role to God. All of Sheldon's editorials examined some aspect of this triple responsibility. Tuesday's editorial examined a person's role to himself or herself and Sheldon as editor; Wednesday's editorial examined person's role to others; cooperating in the spirit of Christian good works; Thursday's editorial examines a person's role to God, salvation. Friday and Saturday's editorials repeat these themes by suggesting the benefits of enacting a contract where a person fulfills his or her responsibility on the preceding three levels.

Friday's editorial on March 16, 1900 concerned "Two great moral issues," liquor and social problems. Sheldon argued that society does not permit murder and suggested John Locke's social contract where people willingly yielded some rights to enjoy the benefit of law. Just as the Ten Commandments are God's law and contributed to the formation of much civil law, Sheldon's idea was that drinking violates the contract of a person's responsibility to himself or herself and others. Resorting to the device of preaching, Sheldon (1900b) warned:

> The man or woman claiming the personal liberty to drink if he pleases because it is no one's business takes upon himself the awful responsibility of helping to keep in existence an universal curse to mankind. That is sin. There is no other word for it in the vocabulary of God's judgment day. And the time is surely hastening on when the world shall see this habit as sin and know that the only way to treat this evil is not simply to be temperate in the use of liquor but to leave it entirely alone. (p. 2)

Again, Sheldon wrote as an Old Testament prophet, warning sin will be punished.

The first item in the list Friday was the liquor problem and the second item was the evil of social problems. In discussing social problems, Sheldon noted that actions are either right or wrong, adding that academics understood that ethics are part of the organizations and systems even in economics. He quoted from I Corinthians 13, often cited as the love chapter, as a solution to the public policy problems of labor and wealth. He ended his editorial by addressing the world as if it were a person, writing, "Take courage old world, groaning under the curse of liquor and man's injustice to man and wrongs to himself! There is a better day coming. The dawn of it is seen in the moral issues that we are beginning to know are moral. God speed the noon day" (Sheldon, 1900f, p. 2).

In this case, Sheldon suggested a subcategory to personal responsibility to others by suggesting the world's role to God. By treating the world as a person, Sheldon floats between the personal response and the public-policy response. He wrote as if he were God, comforting his own creation, but then lapsed into a prayer by eliciting God's intervention in human history, as if to remind God of his contractual obligation to purge the world of its unrighteousness.

Sheldon's fifth editorial Saturday morning, March 17, 1900, was headlined "Four Open Letters" and concerned the Spirit's industry. The first letter condemned the producers of liquor, a person's responsibility to others; the second letter condemned those connected with the trade including publishers who accept alcohol-related advertising and railroad train directors who allowed drinking in their dining cars, a person's responsibility to others. The third letter chastised law enforcement for not making arrests, a person's responsibility to others. The fourth letter, addressed to those who drink, cited a litany of abuses associated with drink, including jail and asylums, a person's responsibility to himself or herself. Sheldon argued that the demand for liquor maintained the interest in the trade. To all those involved, Sheldon urged them to turn to righteousness.

The heart of his argument, while moral, also included the economics of the industry. Sheldon asked, "Who is the greater sinner? The person who sells liquor or the person who drinks it? Let God judge" (Sheldon, 1900c, p. 2). For Sheldon, the judgment is against a business that "ruins manhood and depraves womanhood. It beggars homes, destroys the reason, is mighty and constant as a cause of crime and slays more people every year than the bloodiest war. The evils that come direct from the drink that you are selling for gain have been recognized and denounced by God's word, by courts and authorities of every age" (Sheldon, 1900c, p. 2).

The device of the letter suggests the idea of the epistles in the New Testament where an apostle wrote to a church offering instruction. In Sheldon's letters, he condemned the sin, offered a solution, and ended each letter with a prayer. The hierarchy developed in this editorial goes from those selling liquor, to those making liquor, to those enforcing the laws, to those who consume alcohol. Sheldon asked rhetorically which group was the worse, but did not answer his own question.

In Sheldon's last editorial, the evening of March 17, 1900, he concluded his week of prescriptions to reform individuals, communities, and the world by urging a day of rest. By the end of the series, Sheldon had explained the characteristics of the ideal newspaper, the ideal person, and the ideal world, and this Sunday rest appeal was a way to get readers to think about his thoughts on personal and public responsibility. The contractual benefit of Sunday rest was the chance to think of life differently. Sheldon wrote, "One of the greatest blessings connected with Sunday ought to be the opportunity it affords for a change of thought and a rest for the mind and soul" (Sheldon, 1900j, p. 1). Always the preacher first, Sheldon wanted to end his series with one last appeal for Spiritual Interrogation. He wrote, "Let us give one whole day to God and to heaven . . . " (Sheldon, 1900j, p. 1)."It is entirely possible for Christian civilization to be a great deal more powerful, useful, and intelligent, if everyone would take one whole day in seven to read what he does not read the other days of the week, to think what he does not think during the week, to rest, and pray, and commune with God as he does not during the week" (Sheldon, 1900j, p. 1). The idea of reading what one does not read during the rest of the week apparently did not phase Sheldon as inconsistent or ironic given the goal of his experiment to produce a Christian daily newspaper that would be read on Sundays as well as the rest of the week.

Sheldon believed that individual reform would lead to global reform. His Spiritual Interrogation vision was thoroughly orthodox, but in some ways, it suggested a second fantasy theme. Sheldon believed in Luther's idea of salvation by grace alone, but Sheldon's vision of the ideal world allowed for only homogenized behavior. Good Christians avoided smoking and drinking and responded to appeals to assist in disaster relief such as the famine in India. Somehow good Christians could participate in government without unduly participating in partisan politics. Sheldon is grand with his generalizations but limited in implementing the specifics of his appeals. In his March 15, 1900 editorial, he presented a salvation appeal. Then he told readers to stop selfishness, but he did not provide any specific strategies on stopping selfishness. Just as the Jesus question provides the personal specifics but no absolutes on an issue under scrutiny, Sheldon's vague approach to a plan of action was the hallmark of his rhetorical vision.

For Sheldon, the one issue that seemed to be specifically stated concerned Prohibition. During 1900, five states including Kansas practiced Prohibition. In a certain sense, when Sheldon called for a ban on liquor, he was arguing for a public policy that already existed in his state. To argue for an existing policy is not as dramatic an appeal as it may appear at first brush. Even this issue that received more attention than any other during Sheldon's week as editor and publisher was lacking in specifics. Sheldon did not provide specific suggestions on strategies to alter business or law enforcement policies. In his system, that kind of insight was personal and came from posing the Jesus question. The key was individual response, which would lead to a wider response and finally Heaven on Earth.

The Sheldon edition was an experiment to demonstrate the possibility of inserting Christian ideology into a mainstream, general-circulation newspaper. He applied the approach a Christian periodical would use in writing commentary in a publication with a heterogeneous audience not bounded by ideological considerations. In a sense, Sheldon bent the usual contract between a newspaper editor and reader, that the content would be sanitized of overtly ideological features except the assumptions found in rationalism and science. By presenting the editorial as a series of letters that concluded with an appeal to the divine, Sheldon sough to reform even the convention of the editorial.

An editorial is defined as "area or column in a publication in which the editor or editorial committee/board express views on matters of interest or outline the policy of the publication" (Connors, 1982, p. 86).

Sheldon acted as a one-person committee, who needed only ask himself the Jesus question for answers. By emphasizing the role of an editorial as a kind of letter from the editor to the readers, Sheldon helped unmask ordinary commentary as somehow imbued with incisive insight. Sheldon based his views on the Bible, not rationalism. The timeliness of the Bible and its message of salvation and redemption was the basis of his views. While ordinary editorials talked of reform through changes to the law or other institutions, Sheldon's commentary focused on reform of the heart using the idea that each person is responsible to himself or herself, others and God. This approach finds its best fit in preaching where the preacher's role is to integrate the communing church with its canon (Rice, 1987, p. 494). Rice noted, "From the beginning the church saw an organic relationship to the socioeconomic realm of the *kerygma* (the essential story of life, death, resurrection, and the expected coming of Jesus Christ), and struggled constantly to keep the two differentiated and in their proper relationship" (Rice, 1987, p. 495). The idea is that a preacher has access to transcendent truth that a mere editorial writer may not.

Reaction to the Sheldon Edition

Sheldon wrote in his autobiography that the press reports of his work "were for the most part so misleading even after the week was over that the public never had an opportunity to know what had really been done nor the real results that had been obtained" (1925, p. 125). Sheldon said his critics called his newspaper dull (p. 130). As for *The New York Times*, the opinions expressed in the Sheldon edition represented the kind of content customary in Midwestern newspaper, making the Sheldon edition unremarkable ("Sheldon edition, Editorial comments from papers East and West, Various opinions given, Some do not like scheme of mixing editorials and news–views in general," 1900, p. 6).

In that same article, the *Philadelphia North American* said the experiment should continue much longer and Sheldon would learn that "the public must be interested first, and preached to afterwards" ("Sheldon edition, editorial comments from papers East and West, Various opinions given, Some do not like scheme of mixing editorials and news–views in general," 1900, p. 6). That report went on to say "that a newspaper that deals only in sermons is as far out of the right road as a preacher would be who should read the day's dispatches from his pulpit instead of delivering Christian discourse ("Sheldon edition, editorial comments from papers East and West, Various opinions given, Some do not like scheme of mixing editorials and news–views in general," 1900, p. 6).

The *Montreal Presbyterian Review* wondered if anyone could say how Christ would conduct a newspaper, but that others with Sheldon's goals would produce a very different newspaper ("Sheldon edition, editorial comments from papers East and West, Various opinions given, Some do not like scheme of mixing editorials and news–views in general," 1900n, 6). The *Miami County Record* of Kansas castigated those associated with the Jesus newspaper saying it was repugnant and it "smacks of blasphemy" ("Sheldon edition, editorial comments from papers East and West, Various opinions given, Some do not like scheme of mixing editorials and news–views in general," 1900, p. 6).The *Miami County Record* found Sheldon's lack of specifics on his directives troubling, adding, "Jesus denounced wrong, and He did it without mincing matters. If Mr. Sheldon is to follow *In His Steps* as editor, he must do the same thing ("Sheldon edition, editorial comments from papers East and West, Various opinions given, Some do not like scheme of mixing editorials and news–views in general," 1900, p. 6).

The *Chicago Inter Ocean* criticized the experiment as a money-making ploy where "the sacred name of the Redeemer of Man has been degraded to the purpose of catch-penny advertising and bandied about as a byword and a joke ("Sheldon edition, editorial comments from papers East and West, Various opinions given, Some do not like scheme of mixing editorials and news–views in general," 1900, p. 6). The *St. Louis Globe-Democrat* panned Sheldon's lack of training and wrote, "The Topeka newspaper has been a junk shop of crudities for several days, an exhibit of amateurish fads in sentiment, fancying itself to be something more than a display of the stale, the sloppy and the inexpert" ("Sheldon edition, Editorial comments from papers East and West, Various opinions given, Some do not like scheme of mixing editorials and news–views in general," 1900, p. 6).

The *Philadelphia Times* objected to the idea that ordinary newspapers are not reputable and pointed out that the labor for a Monday newspaper required work on Sunday; however, *The Topeka Daily Capital* did not publish a Monday edition muting this criticism. The *Philadelphia Times* insisted that a daily newspaper "be clean and fit for admission to the family circle. It should be the champion of religion and good morals, as a vast majority of the American newspapers are, but no public journal can be a newspaper according to the limitations put upon it by the severe religionists, for the reason that they reject everything that is not strictly in the interest of religion" ("Sheldon edition, Editorial comments from papers East and West, Various opinions given, Some do not like scheme of mixing editorials and news–views in general," 1900, p. 6).

The *Philadelphia Times* thought the idea of a Jesus newspaper was a good one but Sheldon missed the point. "If Mr. Sheldon, instead of interesting himself as he has in the effort to print and describe what he thinks ought to have happened instead of what actually did happen, if he had edited his newspaper more and Providence less, if he had made the Topeka *Capital* more truthful, more relentlessly accurate, convicted the world of sin by telling the truth about its sins and added to his general exhortation, which never hits anybody, a little of 'thou art the man,' he would really have done what he attempted" ("Sheldon edition, Editorial comments from papers East and West, Various opinions given, Some do not like scheme of mixing editorials and news–views in general," 1900, p. 6).

The *New York Post* said the Sheldon edition inflated the single-copy price, a practice that Christ would not endorse and recommended Sheldon try the experiment for a year or more to determine if a market exist for this kind of content ("Sheldon edition, Editorial comments from papers East and West, What some of the Chicago ministers have to say of the experiment," 1900). The *Lawrence Daily Journal* in Kansas wrote that Sheldon asked the wrong question. "Mr. Sheldon's basic error, which is an unfortunate one, is that he undertakes to do 'what Jesus would do,' instead of trying to do 'what Jesus would have me to do'" ("Sheldon edition, Editorial comments from papers East and West, What some of the Chicago ministers have to say of the experiment," 1900, p. 6). The *Lawrence Daily Journal* also criticized Sheldon for the publishing a news-free newspaper and breaking a basic canon of journalism, suppressing the news.

Following the experiment, even *The Topeka Daily Capital*, while praising Sheldon as a man of integrity, judged his efforts as a editor to be a failure ("The Sheldon edition of the Capital," 1900, p. 4). "It may have a rich miscellany, a broad and intelligent editorial survey of the topics and issues of interest, but if it fails to give the general news from all parts of the world, as well as local and state news, without emasculation and censorship, it fails primarily in giving the people what they want, and have a right to have," ("The Sheldon edition of the Capital," 1900, p. 4). *The Topeka Daily Capital* concluded that demand for a Christian daily does not exist.

Sheldon's fellow clergy were nearly as critical as the press. The Rev. Albert Lazenby of Unity Church in Chicago said that readers demand news, not sermons ("Sheldon edition, editorial comments from papers East and West," 1900, p. 6). The Rev. Dubois H. Loux of Crerar Presbyterian chapel in Chicago accused Sheldon of inconsistency by not following the example of Bishop Edward Hampton, a clergyman who left his congregation to help the needy in the slums using wealth from his literary endeavors (Sheldon, 1984, p. 204). Loux wrote, "Mr. Sheldon is not famous for giving up his congregation to work in the slums, as did one of its (sic) characters, but is known as the editor of a freak newspaper . . . " ("Sheldon edition, editorial comments from papers East and West, What some of the Chicago ministers have to say of the experiment," 1900, p. 6).

Sheldon did receive some praise from his fellow clergy, more for his character than his work with a newspaper. The Rev. John P. Brushingham of First Methodist Church in Chicago, praised Sheldon as an "aggressively good" person who worked for practical unity among churches ("Sheldon edition, editorial comments from papers East and West, What some of the Chicago ministers have to say of the experiment," 1900, p. 9). However, the Rev. James W. Fineld of Warren Avenue Congregational Church in Chicago said the Sheldon edition proved valuable to the cause of Christianity. "The Sheldon edition has done an incalculable amount of good and cannot truthfully be called a failure," ("Sheldon edition, editorial comments from papers East and West, What some of the Chicago ministers have to say of the experiment," 1900, p. 6).

Clergy in St. Louis were more positive. The Rev. Dr. M. Rhodes of St. Mark's English Lutheran Church thought the experiment helped challenge readers and echoed the Social Gospel sentiment of the day: "I have faith enough to believe that we have reached a point of virtue among the people of our land, a longing for something purer and more real for the home, to make such a paper a possibility" ("The Sheldon edition, What ministers, religious papers and the daily press say of it," 1900, p. 9). The Rev. Dr. T.E. Sharp, pastor of Wagoner Place Methodist Episcopal Church, wrote that Sheldon's newspapers were the ideal, "but the idea of a Christian daily newspaper has come to stay" ("The Sheldon edition, What ministers, religious papers and the daily press say of it," 1900, p. 9).

The Rev. Charles L. Kloss, pastor of Webster Groves Congregational Church, approved of the Sheldon edition and disapproved of the clergy who savaged Sheldon's work. Kloss liked Sheldon's innovation of ample bylines, writing, "I like it because reporters and editors sign their names to articles, thus fastening responsibility, and giving play for individual merit" ("The Sheldon edition, What ministers, religious papers and the daily press say of it," 1900, p. 9). In the 1800s, editors often allowed writers to be anonymous to prevent them from commanding much compensation for their prose (Sloan and Startt, 1996, p. 311). However, the use of the byline was used during the Civil War when military generals wanted to identify the reporter of a disputed report and today bylines are routinely used.

The Rev. Cornelius H. Patton, pastor of First Congregational Church, thought the famine relief article appropriate and predicted, "I expect to see many of our papers writing up the India famine, now that Mr. Sheldon has called attention to it" ("The Sheldon edition, What ministers, religious papers and the daily press say of it," 1900, p. 9). In addition to praise for his news selection, other clergy praised the editorials. "His editorials are clean, pure and inspiring," wrote the Rev. Henry Gardner, pastor of Lee Avenue Presbyterian Church ("The Sheldon edition, What ministers, religious papers and the daily press say of it," 1900, p. 9).

The Jesus question troubled Howard S. McAyeal, who was not identified beyond his name. He wrote that Sheldon's ideas, what I referred to as his vision of Spiritual Interrogation, were inadequate. "The question can be satisfactorily answered only when we regard the teaching of Christ as the embodiment of principles and not a category of rules" (The Sheldon edition, What ministers, religious papers and the daily press say of it, 1900, p. 9). He noted that the Sheldon approach is confusing and Sheldon appeared dogmatic on some points and vague on others. The clergy, writers from the religious press, and editors at other newspapers frequently referred to the Sheldon edition as a failure and found Sheldon ill-prepared to perform the duties of an editor. In addition, many said that no one knows what Christ would do as editor. Furthermore, the Rev. Dr. Robert S. McArthur of New York said that Christ shocked many of his day by dining in the house of a publican and offered words of forgiveness of outcast men and women. McArthur wrote, " . . . It is impossible to say what He would do if He were here today" ("The Sheldon edition, What ministers, religious papers and the daily press say of it, 1900, p. 9).

And the *Boston Daily Globe* quoted the late Dwight L. Moody, the celebrated evangelist, who declared in the Tremont temple in 1897, "'I believe if business men (sic) conducted their affairs or if newspapers were run as our churches are conducted they would all be bankrupt in six months'" (The Sheldon edition, What ministers, religious papers and the daily press say of it, 1900, p. 9). Naturally, the Woman's Christian Temperance Union found the Sheldon edition to have been educational and filed an endorsement ("Sheldon issue endorsed," 1900, p. 8).

On March 28, 1900, *The Topeka Daily Capital* offered a final word on the Sheldon edition on its editorial page, and offered some context for the experiment. The unsigned opinion piece said that Sheldon work was meant"to set before his readers the great moral, religious and humanitarian activities of the age instead of the small ephemeral happenings" ("A final word as to the Sheldon paper," 1900, p. 4). The newspaper made allowances for the lack of time and space to properly execute the kind of model Sheldon proposed. The editorial said that Sheldon was expected to produce a revolutionary newspaper in one attempt, when other pioneers are afforded generous amounts of time to fail and try again. Nonetheless, *The Topeka Daily Capital* agreed with the majority that the newspaper was a failure as a newspaper, but it succeeded in awakening interest in religion. "Nothing in many years has done so much to awaken religious interest and to demonstrate the profound religious conviction latent in the world" ("A final word as to the Sheldon paper," 1900, p. 4).

Those that applauded Sheldon's work tended to praise it on the basis that the Jesus newspaper, despite its weakness at providing reports of current events, was still an effort to produce a Christian newspaper. Good Christians had to be for a Jesus newspaper. These supporters were responding to a powerful pull of the fantasy theme. Visions in Symbolic Convergence theory may be righteous, social or pragmatic (Griffin, 1997, p. 38). Sheldon's Spiritual Interrogation vision appealed to supporters who thought that the vision was righteous, highlighting the right and the good even though the newspaper as a product was not very newsy. Supporters rallied around the values associated with the newspaper concept in the abstract, not the actual Sheldon edition. Supporters also responded to the pragmatic vision, not the actual newspaper content, but the vision that a periodical consumed by a diverse audience could lead to widespread conversions and usher in the millennium, Heaven on Earth. The Christian daily newspaper could be the tool by which God could save the world.

Those who rejected the newspaper disapproved along the same basis. To the critics, the Sheldon edition was not righteous as defined in the journalism culture of late nineteenth century. Good newspapers must contain news scrubbed clean of blatant commentary. In part, the Sheldon edition represented a modest threat to the way ordinary mainstream journalism was practiced. The critics indulged in a fantasy theme of their own that says that good journalism is often misunderstood by those who are not in the business. Good journalism reports tragedies. The more tragic, the more newsworthy. Less tragic articles tended to be regarded as lightweight fare. Their fantasy said that knowledge of the grim reality is the best defense to surviving in a world where fate is capricious. Readers must be told what they need to know, even if it is not pleasant, because knowing the day's news is the only way to prepare for the next inevitable tragedy. By shielding readers from bad news and providing commentary-driven reports,

Sheldon was robbing readers of the pleasure of knowing how tragic the world is while the reader went one more day relatively unscathed.

Summary

True to the fictional editor in his novel, Sheldon revolutionized the newspaper policies of his day by rejecting questionable advertising, posting a lists of rules that included the prohibition of profanity and smoking and drinking in the newspaper offices (Lo Bello, 1989, p. 3). He treated disasters as opportunities to give aid to famine victims in India. The response to this appeal led to $100,000 in relief initially and another $90,000 after the newspaper reported the response from readers worldwide (p. 4). The Bible reported crime briefly, Sheldon reasoned, so did his *The Topeka Daily Capital* (p. 5). Even a suicide of a Kansas senator received only a few inches (Sheldon, 1925, pp. 131-132). Church events did not get special treatment but Sheldon did publish articles on the Sermon on the Mount and one headlined, "The Bible: the Basis on Our Christian Civilization" (Lo Bello, 1989, p. 30). Sheldon said he received letters from readers for months after the newspapers were published with some declaring that they had read the Sermon on the Mount for the first time in *The Topeka Daily Capital*.

The excitement the newspaper produced is attributable largely to the novelty of the experiment with Miller (1987, p. 103) calling it "the best-publicized experiment of the entire Social Gospel era." While the increased circulation cannot be denied; however, the correspondents from leading newspapers of the day questioned the experiment (Ek, 1974, p. 25). "The press generally resented the implication that newspapers were un-Christian" (Ek, p. 25). Many considered it dull because it played down crime, scandals, and vice yet Mott, the journalism historian, praised Sheldon, saying, "The inexperienced editor performed, on the whole, a good piece of work in the face of great difficulties" (1941, p. 576). Meanwhile, Hudson, the regular editor of the *Capital* who refused to participate in the experiment, said that he did not believe in the Christian daily idea, and promised that the *Capital* would return to its previous approach, a Republican newspaper (Mott, 1941, p. 576).

Even Sheldon's own denominational publication, *The Congregationalist* of Boston, called the experiment a failure and noted that Jesus "would never have entered upon this experiment" (p. 26). Nonetheless, the revolutionary approach of this newspaper with its new interpretation of news sparked the interests of readers who wrote for copies for nearly two years after Sheldon published his "Sheldon edition" (Lo Bello, 1989, p. 31). In the 1980s *The Topeka Daily Capital* merged with *The Topeka State Journal* and circulation today hovers around 70,000, but the experiment has never been repeated and the excitement over the newspaper "Jesus edited" remains a historical curiosity. Following the experiment, Sheldon could have become an editor but he was disillusioned with the results and said he would never work with newspapers again (Ek, 1974, p. 27). In 1920, however, he became editor-in-chief of the *Christian Herald* and spent four years leading it; ill health forced him to resign as editor, but he remained a contributor for many more years and died in 1946 at the age of 89.

Sheldon's editorials are based on social justice themes and personal Christian experience as suggested by the modernist theology of the nineteenth century. He assumed that God-inspired reform will lead to public policy reform, the result of the interaction of the personal experience with the need to solve societal problems such as alcohol use. He used the fantasy type, a stock idea that members of the group would share, that more factories will make matters only worse. This shared idea helped motivate the audience. His rhetorical vision of people who drink as the most likely group to be involved in crime and wickedness served to unify his audience to share the fantasy. This vision is part of what sustained Sheldon despite news that heaped ridicule on his efforts. He took solace, not in the accolades of others, but in knowing that he was working for the Creator.

Chapter 9

What Are the Lessons from The Jesus Newspaper?

The Rev. Charles M. Sheldon, pastor of Topeka's Central Congregational Church, used his trademark of a list when he spoke to his congregation Sunday, March 18, 1900, saying that he had identified several characteristics of the United States which were making it weak (Lo Bello, 1989, p. 5). He commented on the disregard of keeping the Sabbath holy, one of the Ten Commandments, and then focused on the evil of the liquor trade. Finally, he expressed his alarm over the concentration of wealth in the hands of the few. In the Tuesday, March 20, 1900, *The Topeka Daily Capital*, by then back to its usual "pre-Sheldon" operation, published a report of this sermon along with criticism of the Sheldon edition ("Rev. Mr. Sheldon's Sermon," 1900, p. 6). Although well-meaning, Sheldon was seen as speculating, at best, on the kind of journalism Jesus would practice. However, no newspaper challenged his opinions regarding business, capitalism, and concentrated wealth. The most vitriolic criticism was that Sheldon would allow himself to be connected to so obvious a commercial venture that used the concept of Jesus as editor as little more than a sales gimmick for a circulation drive.

In this examination of Sheldon's work and his editorials, his definition of Christian journalism was explored. While classified as a general-circulation newspaper, Sheldon's newspaper is better understood as a newspaper that advocated a number of social and public policies after the great advocacy press of the day. For instance, it read like a Prohibition newspaper targeted to a readership primarily concerned with temperance issues instead of current news. The temperance reform movement formed the basis for the news selection for this kind of publication. Make no mistake, Sheldon took seriously the idea that the "word" contained power after the biblical idea (Baker, 1961, p. 1).

The manifest content of Sheldon's newspaper concerned the Gospel message of repentance and saving faith, but the subtext for this remarkable experiment, as seen by his editorials, is that no one exists in isolation and everyone has a responsibility to self, others, and God. Sheldon was the relationship editor who urged his flock of readers to possess ideal relationships with God, other Christians, community institutions, and others. In this system, journalism for Sheldon was defined as "anything in the way of daily events that the public ought to know for its development and power for a life of righteousness" (1900l, p. 2). He printed news, which represented what he considered scandalous behavior, but he deferred the details on the principle that it is more polite to be general and to hint at personal misconduct rather than make a clear denunciation of a sin in general. For instance, Sheldon would not use his position as the relationship editor to castigate a member of the Topeka community for drunkenness; however, he would use the bully pulpit of his editorials to denounce alcohol creation and use.

The pattern in his six editorials was to be very directive as well. Sheldon told his readers to seek an ideal relationship with God; he told the press to seek an ideal relationship with readers. He told Christians to seek an ideal relationship with other Christians, and he told readers to seek an ideal relationship with the community.

A product of his time, Sheldon's vision revealed his pre-World War I conviction tempered by the Social Gospel that the world was evolving into a better place and a Christian daily newspaper could help usher in God's kingdom on Earth if people assumed the right relationships. The ideal was possible and inevitable. In Sheldon's vision, all of life was a matter of polar opposites. On alcohol use, two positions were possible–Prohibition or drunkenness. No middle ground existed. As for time, two positions were possible–Sunday as a day of rest or Sunday as an ordinary day. This simple view of stark contrasts reduced life to a bland middle-class world where all of life's problems could be captured in the action of a melodramatic novel. Sin amounted to drinking alcohol. Complications such as alcohol-based medicines did not factor into Sheldon's system, and, therefore, did not exist.

This tidy approach to life included the press, which could serve one of two functions–promote relationships or promote greed. In Sheldon's world, right relationships automatically led to selflessness. Information without some compelling purpose was second-rate. Like the blatant entertainment coverage that was banned in his newspaper, information that appeared to titillate, such as reports of scandals, could not have a redeeming purpose. For Sheldon, then, journalism was defined by specific issues, particularly morality issues such as temperance. News as the summary of the day's events was not the operating definition for Sheldon.

In many ways Sheldon's attempt at a Christian daily was noble, but the execution was paternalistic. Sheldon's vision did not allow for mature reactions to life where a person could have a thoughtful response to information beyond the Sheldon directive. Sheldon saw readers as easy to influence after a kind of inoculation approach where a uniform reaction would occur by all who were exposed to the message. The Christian daily Sheldon fashioned was more about being effective and less about engaging the cognitive. His press was too directive, too narrowly focused and lacking in an appreciation for the reader's ability to process complicated material. For Sheldon, journalism was defined as providing the right answer, not the process of arriving at it.

For Sheldon, the Jesus question suggested uniformity and closure; however, then as today, asking questions often provoked more questions. Asking a charged question such as "What would Jesus do?" can only lead to less closure, not more. Sheldon's Spiritual Interrogation was meant to make answers to life's questions more accessible, but his vision diluted the mystery and power of a person's journey to meet God and grapple with the human condition with freshness. Sheldon's vision of "one size fits all" did not allow for the beauty of Christian liberty in the face of vexing challenges. Many of his ideas were biblically sound, such as the contractual idea of blessings, but his approach to the press was flawed by his attention to quick solutions for age-old problems such as war.

The criticism of fantasy theme analysis in general is its cyclical emphasis on solidarity (Griffin, 1997, p. 38). Group fantasy is said to lead to the groups coming together by providing a vision with motives that impel the believers to act out the vision. For the convergence to occur, solidarity must be pre-existing. Nonetheless, the fantasy theme demonstrates that people are symbol-using creatures bounded primarily by the need to tell a story, a narrative, that involves some kind of fantasy at its heart. The method works as well for mass communication as it does for small group interaction (Bormann, 1985, p. ix). This study used the humanistic tradition to gain insight into the symbolic interaction of the human condition. It relied on a close reading of Sheldon's words, images and ideas in the historic context to learn about this era in journalism history.

When conducting this kind of interpretative analysis, it can be argued that preconceived ideas were read into the text. The goal was to allow the vision to surface from Sheldon's own work. This study examined Sheldon's work by examining the bigger issue of the universal pattern of symbol-using. It attempted to examine the more specific issue of the Sheldon artifact in a new way to provoke appreciation for his work. Finally, it tried to explore the assumptions that guide Christians who want to use the press as a tool for spreading the Gospel.

The Sheldon edition raised awareness for reform issues and Christianity's benefits to the world. However, Sheldon could have done so much more if he had kept the course that he started with his novels, particularly *In His Steps*. Sheldon gained an audience by telling a story. That's a function of a good newspaper—story telling. Today the best newspapers present the news narrative in the most compelling way possible. "What would Jesus do?" as an editor? I suspect he would do what he did when he preached. He told parables, stories. The parables entertained first, then taught. The listeners could relate to the characters, plots and settings for the specifics in a way making a general statement of principle cannot do. Sheldon was a story-teller but he allowed the format of a newspaper to distract him from the gift that made him such a popular writer. *In His Steps* remains a classic among Christians today as a way for believers to learn about the faith from a narrative.

The Sheldon experiment prompts the question, "Is Christianity as an organizing system for journalism an appropriate model?"

Experiments continue.

On the national level, *The National Courier* attempted a modern-day version of Sheldon's *The Topeka Daily Capital*. The *National Courier* was a publication of Dan Malachuk's Logos International Fellowship, the world's largest charismatic book publisher of the 1970s (Keeler, Tarpley and Smith, 2000, p. 279). The newspaper published between 1975 and 1977. In a promotional brochure, Chief Editor Bob Slosser, said the *National Courier* would look for trends, insist on telling the truth even about fellow Christians, but seek to edify (p. 279). In addition, the newspaper would explain to readers what stories meant. The editorial page would be clearly marked and reserved for overt preaching. "We are not a Jesus paper, but a religious journal" (p. 281). The concept of the publication was to produce a newspaper to cover the whole spectrum of events to meet the needs of the whole man, as one *National Courier* staff member put it. However, the newspaper failed for lack of adequate paid circulation.

In a small town near Gettysburg, a semi-weekly, general circulation newspaper has bent Sheldon's approach to blend traditional news in its regular newspaper and "uplifting" stories in a monthly supplement (Smith, 1992, p. 9). The 6,500 circulation of the mainstream *News-Chronicle* newspaper began publishing in 1844 in Shippensburg, Pennsylvania, and its religion pages include sermons, commentary, book reviews and columns that emphasize the deity of Christ and a salvation message.

Another example of a Christian initiative is *World* magazine, which provides a weekly summary of world news and commentary from a Christian perspective (Belz, 1994, p. 5). From a false-start in 1986 and then a renewed attempt in 1987, *World* is published 50 times a year. It has about 120,000 subscribers. According to the figures from the year *2000 Standard Rate and Data Sheet*, circulation is as follows: *Time*, 4.1 million; *Newsweek*, 3.14 million; *U.S. News and World Report*, 2.1 million. With *World*'s 120,000 subscribers, its circulation is larger than *The New Republic*, 95,713; *The Nation*, 97,213; *The Weekly Standard*, 49,460; or *Insight*, 60,954, four magazines considered to have similar opinion-oriented missions to that of *World*.

Each issue of *World* publishes its mission statement:

> To report and analyze the news on a weekly schedule in an interesting, accurate, and arresting fashion, and to combine reporting with practical commentary on current events and issues from a perspective committed to the Bible as the inerrant Word of God.

World is Christocentric, and seeks to show:

> . . . how man without God is a beast, by showing how Christians can make a difference by putting biblical precepts into practice, by showing the difference between the fraudulent pretensions of some Christians and the real thing, by exposing anti-Christian leaders and programs, by showing how individuals can glorify God even in Babylon, by showing how Christians enjoy what God has given ... (Olasky, 1996, p. 31).

In addition to this magazine, about 30 Christian weekly
newspapers are published in the United States. According to the
Christian Newspaper Association in Minneapolis, an organization that
helps these publications with national advertising and other issues,
these newspapers are vigorous, but their budgets are small. When the
Christian Newspaper Association gathers for its annual meeting, the
idea of a national Christian newspaper is among the topics debated. The
hope is that someday the resources will allow an enterprising publisher
to sustain circulation and make a profit in the twenty-first century.

Carey's (1989) idea that ritualistic communication is superior to
transmission of information and helps explain the formation of reality
for people. In mass media, the content of news need not vary drastically
to fulfill the ritualistic function of information that is routine, familiar,
and comforting. The names and places in the news may change, but the
basic conflicts reported do not and this dynamic provides an audience
with a sense that despite the tragedies and crimes, all is well. As in
religion, the ritual has symbolic significance. The ritual also reflects
the need for a community to be reminded of the shared ideas, beliefs
and values in a society, as in the shared elements that are articulated in
a weekly sermon from the clergy.

Experiments in advocacy publishing such as the *National Courier*,
The News Chronicle, and *World* fulfill the ritualistic function of the
press; however, they go beyond that level of predictable content to
emphasize a strident ideological message. The Sheldon edition, while a
historic curiosity, provided a world view that all these publications tend
to share; but few general-circulation newspapers have succeeded in
maintaining a Christocentric worldview. That was key to Sheldon who
said that some readers told him that it was the publication of his
Sermon on the Mount article that led them to a salvation (Lo Bello,
1989, p. 31).

Often overlooked in Sheldon's experiment are the journalistic
breakthroughs that readers take for granted today. Sheldon insisted that
news reporters sign their work. The last mainstream newspaper to
abandon the no-byline policy was The *Williamsport Sun-Gazette* in
February 1990. John E. Persons, president of the newspaper at the time,
said, "We consider the publication to be the byline, not the individual"
(Smith, 1990, p. 29). The use of a byline for all journalistic enterprise
provides some recognition for the creator of the artifact and imbues the
work with some pride of ownership. It allows the reader to know the
identity of the person who is responsible for the work. In this way, one
small part of Sheldon's rhetorical vision succeeded in saturating the
craft of journalism. The role of the individual was elevated. Personal

response could still be exercised by the simple act of attaching a byline to a journalistic product.

Perhaps the greatest contribution that Sheldon made was his insistence on truthfulness in advertising. At the turn of the century, businesses routinely made gross exaggerations and misleading claims (Ault, Emery, 1997, p. 420). It was not until 1911 that the Truth in Advertising law was passed. In 1913, the Better Business Bureau was organized to promote ethical practices among business. In 1914, the Audit Bureau of Circulations was formed to issue unbiased audits of periodicals. In 1931, the Supreme Court ruled that the Federal Trade Commission, reestablished in 1914, could restrict deceptive advertising when it hurt competition. Then in 1938, the FTC banned advertisements that deceive consumers.

Sheldon was ridiculed during the week of his experiment for his strict policy on advertising. Sheldon said that he read every line of advertising copy (Sheldon, 1925, pp. 121-122). For instance, he changed one advertisement for Topeka Laundry Company that read, "Strictly high grade work" to "Claims to do strictly high grade work" (Ripley, 1965, p. 21). Sheldon avoided any advertisements whose truthfulness he could not verify, hence the ban on patent medicine. This high standard anticipated newspaper convention of today where display advertising departments screen advertisements that promise exaggerated benefits. In 1936, Houston, one of Sheldon's advertising agents during his week as newspaper editor, suggested the truth-in-advertising movement may have begun at *The Topeka Daily Capital* in 1900 (pp. 15-16). Houston was posthumously elected to the Advertising Hall of Fame in 1957.

Summary

As stated earlier in this chapter, in this examination of Sheldon's work, primarily his editorials, the research question examined Sheldon's definition of applied Christianity in a general-circulation newspaper. Journalism can be defined as serving the public good (Altschull, 1990, p. 359), and Sheldon supported this idea as an editor who urged readers to seek ideal relationships as the highest good. In addition, journalism as defined by Sheldon meant embracing directives on issues that he considered non-negotiable–for example, temperance. Finally, journalism was defined as information that lead to the right decision or reaction, which would lead to selflessness, the highest of Christian ethical ideals. Sheldon saw as the *telos* of life, the *summum bonum*, to be in a right relationship with the Creator. His journalism espoused this idea and suggested that readers who pose the Jesus question will gain automatic insight into all of life's questions. The

Jesus question was the way to search for the *Good* that Aristotle longed to find. Sheldon's newspaper provided ready-made answers to the vexing questions of the day such as the use of alcohol; and this quality, more than any others, defined his news approach as advocacy journalism. However, by practicing advocacy journalism, Sheldon defeated the goal of his experiment to create a revolutionary model for journalism that remains within the conventions of the mainstream general-circulation press.

To be effective, journalism for the general-circulation press must provide the grit and detail that helps a reader vicariously experience the report. A full telling of all the day's news is the only way anyone will gain an appreciation for the complex world in which only a supernatural Creator can provide supernatural solutions. Nonetheless, future research must examine the link between faith and news. Another experiment in the twenty-first century may help Christians who want to offer an alternative to the press conventions of today. Rosen (1996) argued that journalists today must no longer play observers only and must contribute to solutions facing the American nation, a return to the advocacy model. Sheldon's approach is consistent with this community journalism model. Somewhere on the spectrum of modern mainstream journalism exists a place for journalism inspired by faith. For this kind of experiment to work, the elements used by Sheldon with his emphasis on relationships, responsibility, and results might be considered before launching a publication said to be edited by Jesus.

Furthermore, the idea of Jesus as an editor must be re-thought. What would Jesus do as a physician? Heal the sick. What would Jesus do as a farmer? Provide food. What would Jesus do as an editor? No glib answers readily come to mind. For sure Jesus would insist on high-quality story telling. I think he would want journalists to cover the world with depth and compassion. I suspect the articles that Jesus would endorse would be colorful and filled with relevant details that provoke readers to ponder the ordinary and the extraordinary. To produce a quality newspaper, a better approach may be to examine the notion of public service and evaluate the search for the *Good* from Sheldon's original perspective of seeking ideal relationships, first with the Creator and then with the community. The press today does not provide much that demonstrates the hand of the Supernatural at work in the world. And that feature, more than any other, can make any newspaper a vehicle that points readers to Christ; however, the best way to engage a reader is to return to Sheldon's first approach based on the way Jesus presented his messages—story telling. We are a story-telling people and the news that can entertain and delight while informing and provoking reform will go a long way to achieving the kind of press Sheldon yearned to see in his day.

Appendix

The editorials of the Sheldon edition

Editor's note:
Full-Text Reprints of Charles M. Sheldon's Editorials with the
punctuation and grammar used in the original
The Topeka Daily Capital Tuesday, March, 13, 1900

Editorial 1

The Topeka Capital This Week

Tuesday, March 13, 1900, Page 2, Editorial Page

Last December the owners of *The Topeka Daily Capital* asked me to assume entire charge of the paper for one week and edit it as a distinctly Christian daily.

I have accepted the invitation on condition that I receive no financial compensation and share of the profits be used for some benevolent work, and named the week beginning Tuesday, March 13, 1900, as the week for the experiment. With the hearty co-operation of every person connected with the paper and with the help of the wisdom that I have prayed might be given me from Him who is wiser than any of us, I shall do the best I can.

If a thousand different Christian men who wished to edit Christian dailies should make an honest attempt to do so, the result might be a thousand different papers in very many particulars. In other words, these Christian editors might arrive at different conclusions in the interpretation of what is Christian. It is, of course, the farthest from my purpose to attempt to show in a dogmatic way what is the one thing that Jesus would do in every case. The only thing I or any other Christian man can do in the interpretation of what is Christian in the conduct of this paper is to define the term Christian the best that can be done after asking for divine wisdom, and not judge others who might with equal desire and sincerity interpret the probable action of Jesus in a different manner.

With this understanding of the conduct of the paper this week, I will state in part its general purpose and policy.

1. It will be a news paper. The word "news" will defined as anything in the way of daily events that the public ought to know for its development and power for a life of righteousness. Of necessity the editor of this paper, or of any other with this definition of "news," will determine not only the kind, but the quantity of any particular events that ought to be printed. The importance of one kind of "news" compared with another kind will also determine the place in the paper where matter will be printed. If it seems to the editor that certain subjects representing great causes that belong to the profoundest principles of human life are the most important, they will be given the first page of the paper whether are telegraphic items or not. It might easily become the settled policy of a permanent paper similar to this one, to consider the detailed account of an unusual battle as of less importance to the reader than an account of the usual daily destruction being caused by liquor. The first page of the Capital this week will contain what seems to the editor to be the most vital issues that affect humanity as a whole.

2. The paper will be non-partisan, not only in municipal and state politics, but also in national politics. I do not mean to say that a Christian daily can not be partisan. This is simply my interpretation of Christian as applied to this part of the paper's life.

3. On the liquor question the paper will advocate the prohibition of the whole liquor business from Maine to California and all around the globe. By Prohibition I mean the total extinction of the curse of making, selling, buying and drinking intoxicating liquor: its extinction by legal enactment, by personal total abstinence, and by every form of state, home, church and school education that Christians can devise.

4. The great social questions of the age will be given prominence. The selfishness of mankind in every form of greed, commercially or politically, will be considered as of more serious consequences to us as a people than many other matters which too often engage the time and attention of mankind.

5. The paper will declare its abhorrence of war as it is being waged today not only in Africa but in the Philippines and everywhere else.

6. On matters of "finance" or "tariff" or "expansion," matters of public concern which have to do with measures of this character, the editor has personal opinion which may or may not be voiced in this paper. If he gives expression to them it will be in no dogmatic or positive manner, as if he knew what the whole Christian truth was concerning them. In regard to many of these questions I do not know what is the Christian answer to them. In regard to others, my study of them has not yet resulted in convictions that are strong enough to print.

I do not wish to declare through this paper a policy concerning certain political measures which are not clear in my own mind.

7. The main purpose of the paper will be to influence readers to seek first the Kingdom of God. A nation seeking the Kingdom of God first of all, will in time find right answers to all disputed questions and become a powerful and useful nation.

8. Editorials, and other articles, written by reporters, will be signed by writers. The exceptions will be small items and such local and telegraphic news as in its nature does not require signature.

9. There will be no Sunday paper, but instead a Saturday evening edition suitable for Sunday reading.

I wish to take this opportunity to thank the many friends everywhere who have been impossible for me to answer them personally. I also wish to express to the host of Christian correspondents who have sent me assurances of their prayers for this week's work, my deep acknowledgement of the source of whatever strength I have felt in preparing for a task which lies beyond the reach of any merely human effort.

May God bless the use of this paper to the glory of His Kingdom on the earth.

CHARLES M. SHELDON

Editorial 2

What can we do to make this a better city?

Wednesday, March, 14, 1900, Page 2, Editorial Page

First, we can all be better men and women ourselves. It does not make any great difference so far as the character of the city is concerned whether we personally belong to one political party or another; whether we are artistic, or musical, or college educated, or ignorant, or wealthy, or poor, will not make any great difference necessarily with the moral condition of the city. But it will make a great and vital difference if we are better men and women every day. It is for more important to this city that we tell the truth, and keep pure, and act unselfishly, and love one another, than that we build factories and encourage commercial industries, and put up fine residences and improve our property. It is as true now as it was when the words were first spoken, that "righteousness exalteth a nation; but sin is a reproach to any people." "See ye first the Kingdom of God and all these things shall be added unto you."

If Topeka is, first of all, a city full on men and women who want to do God's will instead of their own, who are seeking the Kingdom of God before they seek first their own wealth or political honor and social place, the city will be worth more in everything else that makes a city that it ought to be. What we need more of than anything else in this city, (and the same is true of every other city in the world), is better people, more personal righteousness of the kind that stands the wear and tear of the business life and the social and political life of the municipality.

Another thing that we can all do to make a better city is to conduct our municipal politics on non-partisan lines. It is a childish thing for grown up men and women to try to conduct the business administration of the city on a partisan basis. A business man who ran his business on lines marked out by partisan municipal politics would be regarded by all sane business men as lacking the most necessary common sense. And yet cities full of business men continue to try to run the business of cities as they never would allow their own to be conducted. Why don't we all get together like sensible men and say, "The men we need for city offices are men who understand the business who have honest, personal character of a high order, and fitness to do the duties of the places to which they are elected." What difference does it make whether they belong to one party or another? What difference does it make whether they believe in gold or silver money? If they are good, honest, capable citizens who will administer the offices to the best interests of all the people in the city, that is enough. This is about all that is necessary to say about non-partisanship in municipal affairs. It is very simple and we shall begin to have a better city as soon as we act out what a majority of us already believe in our hearts is the sensible thing to do.

We can help to make a better city by ceasing to criticize (sic) one another so much.

It is an age of criticism. No matter what a man proposes to do to better things, somebody is sure to rise up and begin to ask questions and get in the way of progress or find fault because it isn't done in some other way. If Gabriel or some other angel should be sent directly from heaven to start a movement for helping to make this a better city and if he brought plans right from his own home and had no other object in view except to bless as many of us as possible, somebody would probably come forward and try to serve an injunction on him, or suggest plans that were drawn by some one more versed in practical philanthropy than an angel. What is the matter with us that we don't work more and criticize less? And in addition to this spirit of criticism we also judge one another without knowing the facts in the case. We need to do away with this spirit of criticism and judging before our city will be better.

There is also here and in every other city a great opportunity for all the forces of righteousness to come together and act together for the common good of all. Our different church denominations are on very friendly terms. The sixty-five separate church organizations in Topeka are ready, in a large, and I believe, a very Christian spirit, to cooperate in making conditions more righteous. But there is a great deal more we might do by getting into one federated organization every sect and denomination in order to make a better municipality. Where the churches could not agree in the matter of creed, or dogma, or ritual, they could easily agree even more than they do, on the great common needs of humanity. Righteousness is not sectarian. The temperance cause does not have a denominational watch-word. Purity and honesty and fair dealing between man and man, and love of one's neighbor, are elemental things, that all men can unite upon for the common good of the human family.

We can have a better city if we want it. It lies wholly in our power to make this city a place that God shall delight to honor with that prosperity which is worth while because it is the result of personal righteousness. Let us all do our share to make this city what it ought to be.

CHARLES M. SHELDON

Editorial 3

The world's greatest need

Thursday, March, 15, 1900, Page 2, Editorial Page

If Jesus were here again facing the very civilization that we face, and seeing in detail all that we see, living the life that we live now, what would be His answer in the question of the world's greatest need? What would He preach about oftenest? What texts would He use? What central truth would He emphasize?

It is easy to see Jesus facing a multitude of all sorts and conditions of men of this generation and saying to them identically the same things He said to the age into which He was born. It would not surprise us if the first sermon He preached to a congregation here in Topeka or anywhere else would have for its text: "Repent." Or possibly the old words, "Ye must be born again." Or, "Seek ye first the Kingdom of God."

If this is true, if Jesus would preach, more than anything else, the need of a regenerated humanity, then that is the greatest need of the world. I do not mean to say that He would not use any other texts or words. The very fact of this great need would compel preaching about the detailed selfishness which makes the need itself. It is not easy to conceive of Christ keeping silent on the liquor question as it faces us, or saying nothing about the greed of much of the modern business life, or the horrors of war, or the injustice of man to man in his commercial relations. He would undoubtedly speak in detail against those sins. But He would do so because the one great need of all humanity is regeneration of life. The new heavens and the new earth wherein "dewelleth righteousness" will be possible when men are born again.

Selfishness is at the bottom of all the world's trouble. There is not a social wrong, there is not a ruined home, there is not a tangled condition of life anywhere, that does not have for its real cause a selfish life. The greatest need for the world is to get rid of this horrible selfishness. It is the sin of all the generations. And as fast as it is taken away by the power of Christ, as He is allowed to come into the daily life, so fast will the life of men on the earth become the happy, strong, beautiful life that God longs to have it. The greatest need of Topeka, of Kansas, of the United States, of the whole world, is a regenerated humanity.

CHARLES M. SHELDON

Editorial 4

Moral Issues
Friday, March, 16, 1900, page 2, Editorial Page

There are two great morals issues before the whole today.

For the sake of definition they may be called "The Liquor Problem" and "The Social Problem."

Every one acknowledges the moral issue in the liquor problem. Every day the line grows more sharply defined between the man who drinks and the man who does not. Every day arrays on one side or the other more positively the friends and the enemies of the liquor traffic. Every day adds to the curse connected with both the making and using in any form the stuff that kills the true life of both maker and user.

If has been said that the saloon does not present as sharp an issue as slavery. The appetite for drink, it is said, is not a thing that can be legislated out of existence as slavery was. There is no Lincoln for the temperance cause to write a proclamation of emancipation declaring all souls free from the liquor bondage. Men will not be free. They choose to bind themselves to this matter.

That is true. And still, slavery never presented more definite and clear cut reasons for being abolished than the liquor business presents. There is a moral issue here that has no comparison or explanation can lessen. And as time goes on and civilized nations try one form and another of restriction and suppression or license of this sin, it grows more evident that the only answer to the whole evil is its extermination. We do not license murder or theft or arson or perjury for so much a year. We do not pass laws authorizing our states through their salaried agents to collect legal revenue from those who are committing acts that result in crime and poverty and disgrace and impurity. Why do we civilized people of the world continue to suppose that we can treat a sin like a legitimate business and escape from the legitimate consequences?

All forms of license, government control, state agencies or systems that connect the liquor business with the state as a recipient of its gains are not facing the moral issue that lies back of all the liquor problem itself. The liquor business is a sin. The saloon is a gigantic evil. There is no other treatment of a sin except to take it away. There is no other remedy for an evil except to wipe it out.

That is the reason we are Prohibitionists in Kansas. We believe that an institution that has done as much harm as the saloon ought not to have an existence of any sort. We believe that a wrong thing ought not to be licensed or recognized by the state as a business under any specious plea of supervision or control. We believe that the only supervision the state has any right to exert over the liquor business is the supervision of an undertaker over a corpse that need to be buried as quick as possible.

There is also demonstrating the other truth that the drinker as well as the seller is a sinner. For a soul made in God's image deliberately to use a thing that is so saturated with the sin of the world is certainly an awful use of free choice. The sin that the drinker commits may not be outwardly so clear and gross in its manifestations as the sin of the man who sells the liquor. And yet it would be a terrible question for the drinker to have to face as he may some time, (as he is facing it every day), "How far have my own drinking habits perpetuated and encouraged this world sin of the ages?" The man or woman claiming the personal liberty to drink if he pleases because it is no one's business takes upon himself the awful responsibility of helping to keep in existence a universal curse to mankind. That is a sin. There is no other word for it in the vocabulary of God's judgment day. And the time is surely hastening on when the world shall see this habit as a sin and know that the only way to treat this evil is not simply to be temperate in the use of liquor but to leave it entirely alone. There is no way to "supervise" this personal sin except to kill it and bury it.

The moral issue in the Social Problem is as real as that in the Liquor Problem but it has not been so real to the looker on not even to the student of social questions. It is, however, growing more clear every day that all so called economic questions are first of all moral questions. The subjects that are being discussed today by real seekers after the truth in the Social Problem, are questions that openly and frankly acknowledge the great presence of those words "right," and "wrong," in connection with all man's relations to man. A professor in political economy can not ignore the ethics of his department without leaving out the most important factor in it. A book on any phase of the Social Problem that does not discuss the moral obligations of men is a useless book. It might as well be a compilation of geometrical figures so far as being of any real value to economics is concerned.

It is a hopeful sign of the times that men are beginning to see this truth. The study of social questions which has been conducted in the fog and mist of unknown and vague terms of the class room as "economics," is at last becoming clear to the world as simply right conduct between men who are related in business and in social life everywhere to one another. The Sermon on The Mount is the best text book on the Social Problem ever printed. The Golden Rule and the Thirteenth Chapter of I Corinthians are worth more as real solutions to all the perplexities of "labor" and "wages" and "capital" and "distribution," than all the volumes that men have written in the last twenty-five years. That is because the Social Problem is a moral problem and nothing but a remedy that emphasizes a moral answer can answer it.

Take courage, old world, groaning under the curse of liquor and man's injustice to man and wrongs to himself! There is a better day coming. The dawn of it is seen in the moral issues that we are beginning to know are moral. God speed the noon day!

CHARLES M. SHELDON

Editorial 5

Four open letters

Saturday morning, March, 17, 1900, Page 2, Editorial Page

NO. 1. To Those Who Make and Sell Intoxicating Liquors

Whether you are selling illegally, as in the state of Kansas and other prohibitory states, or whether you are selling by permission of some license law, makes no difference so far as the liquor is concerned. The drink that you sell from an illegal joint or over the bar of a palatial licensed saloon is the stuff that ruins manhood and depraves womanhood. It beggars homes, destroys the reason, is mighty and constant as a cause of crime and slays more people every year than the bloodiest wars. The evils that come direct from the drink that you are selling for gain have been recognized and denounced by God's word, by courts and authorities of every age. The curses that have flowed from your traffic are so terrible that it seems almost incredible that humanity can any where be engaged in the drink business as a business. What will you answer to the God of all the earth when you come up before Him for judgment, ye brewers and whisky dealers, ye saloonkeepers and jointists, as each one of you faces the question, "Where is they brother?" If for the sake of gain ye have destroyed your brother, how can that gain be enjoyed by you? May the Lord God Omnipotent by His searching of your conscience and heart turn you from the unholiest business that ever man entered and convict you of slaying your fellow man for greed.

NO. 2. To Those Who Are Connected With the Liquor Business Commercially and Politically

You are not making and selling intoxicating drink, but how about your connection with it in a business way? How about that whisky or champagne advertisement in your paper or magazine? You accept it because it is good pay. How much does it close your mouth against the

traffic? How about that railroad train on the road of which you are
a president or director where liquor is served in a dining car and where
the freight business in liquor is so large a financial figure that your
employes (sic) on the road understand that if they agitate privately
against the liquor business, they risk the loss of their positions? How
about that business block that you own or control which you have
rented to a saloon or sold to a jointist because the property is not
profitable for something else? How about that vote that you have cast
for license because you are commercially interested in the drink
business and can not afford to lose patronage or lose standing with your
party?

The taint of drink money is on your fingers. You are guilty with the
men who make and sell the accursed stuff. And surely God will judge
you all together.

NO. 3. To Those Who Are Authorized to Enforce the Law

The law is greater than fear. But too many of you have made it less.
Or, caring nothing for your solemn oaths of office you have dishonored
the dignity of the state tad the statute. Where are your courage and your
manhood? Is it nothing to you that a sovereign people in this state stand
back of the enacted law and bid you enforce it? It is not for you to
interpret the law or excuse yourselves for lack of power. All honor to
those officials who at risk of scorn and venom and political loss and the
opposition even of courts of justice, that should have helped instead of
hindered the law's enforcement, have nevertheless done their simple
duty. There are such men in Kansas, and there will be many more of
them in the future if we educate our children aright to love God and the
law. Stand fast to your oaths of office, men! Ye who have that sacred
duty to fulfill, be true to it in the name of God and the state!

NO. 4. To Those Who Drink Intoxicating Liquor

Who is the greater sinner? The man who sells liquor or the man
who drinks it? Let God judge. But so far as the curse itself is
concerned, some one desired to drink before any one could be induced
to sell. My brother, do you drink even a little? I do not ask, do you get
drunk, or do you frequent saloons joints or hotel bars? But do you drink
at all? Then you are making possible the breweries, the distilleries, the
saloons, the house of ill fame, the asylums, the penitentiaries of the
world. For they all go together. How can you endure the awful burden
of being a cause of this earth curse? For as long as you continue to
drink you create a demand for the manufacture and sale. What will be
your excuse before the throne of God in the last great day? Will you
dare say you had a personal right to drink, and it was nobody's
business? But how then will you disconnect your own habit from the
fact that because you had it, other men made and sold the stuff and

other men lied and sold their souls for gain in the business of it, and others murdered and stole and assaulted for the sake of it, of that which you helped to keep in existence because you claimed your right to drink regardless of your weaker brother. The Lord have mercy on you and turn you towards righteousness. For you are guilty before Him in the matter of this awful sin under which the world groans today, even after two thousands years of the Blessed Christ the Son of God.
CHARLES M. SHELDON

Editorial 6

The Saturday evening edition
Saturday evening, March, 17, 1900, Page 1

We read in the Bible that God rested after the work of the creation, and declared that this rest period was to be observed by the human race.

The great wisdom of this divine command has never been questioned by the most thoughtful men and women. The reasons why we need a regular recurring period of rest for body and mind are so many and so sensible that they are practically self evident. Disobedience to the command has always resulted in loss to nations and individuals. Obedience to it has always resulted in blessing to nations and individuals.

It is with a very profound belief in the value of this one day out of seven that this particular issue of the Capital has been published. Out of the greatest blessings connected with Sunday ought to be the opportunity it affords for a change in thought and a rest for mind and soul. On this account there is no news of the world published in this issue. The human race can be just as happy and useful and powerful if it does not know every twenty-four hours the news of the wars and sports and the society events of the world. Let us give God a fair opportunity to reach our souls by turning from the six days of our earthly struggles which we call history, and letting our religious natures have a whole day in which to grow and express themselves. For we are religious before we are intellectual or artistic. Our souls are more importance than our bodies. Let us give one whole day to God and to heaven, and to our Christian relations to our neighbor. We shall not lose anything if we do not know until Monday or even the next day what the world has been doing. It is not fair to shut out of our lives so much, Him who made us to live to His glory on earth.

It is entirely possible for Christian civilization to be a great deal more powerful, useful and intelligent, if everyone would take one whole day in seven to read what he does not read the other days of the week, to think what he does not think during the week, to rest, and pray, and commune with God as he does not during the week. We have too much humanity, if that is all we are willing to have. We need more divinity to make our lives complete.

It is hardly necessary for me to say that this particular kind of a paper for Sunday use might be varied in such as way as to bring to its readers each Saturday night a quantity of reading matter of great value. I have used the Bible for this one issue as an illustration of what might be done for every week in the year. I would have a different paper each time. The one aim kept in view each time would be to give the public something entirely different from the other issues of the paper. The editor of a daily paper ought not to be afraid to give his readers one paper during the week that would be distinctly religious. A special editor to take charge of this one number could find plenty of good material for the fifty-two weeks in the year and the amount of good that might be done by that last issue of each week is incalculable. The same plan could be pursued with an evening as with a morning paper. On that account if I were in charge of a Christian daily of my own I would choose an evening paper.

There has been no Sunday work done on this paper. The press and mailing work stopped before midnight of Saturday. The carriers were instructed to deliver their papers in time to reach home themselves before Sunday. There will be no papers sold or delivered on Sunday with the approval of the editor.

May God bless the use of the press of the world to the glory of His Kingdom on earth.

CHARLES M. SHELDON

References

Addams, J. (1909). *The spirit of youth and the city streets.* New York: Macmillan.

Agee, W. K., Ault, P. H. and Emery, E. (1997). *Introduction to Mass Communication, 11th Ed.* New York: Harper Collins College Publishers.

Altschull, J. H. (1990). *From Milton to McLuhan, the ideas behind American Journalism.* New York: Longman.

Allitt, P. (1993, Fall). John Lukacs and the idea of history. *The Intercollegiate Review,* 20-27.

Baker, R. T. (1961). *The Christian as a journalist.* New York: Association Press.

Babize, A. (1935). *Fifty years after: The class of 1885,* Williams College. Privately published.

Baldasty, G. J. (1992). *The commercialization of news in the nineteenth century.* University of Wisconsin Press: Madison.

Beasley, M., and Ward, D. (1993, Summer-fall).What should a Ph.D. student in media history study? *American Journalism, 10,* 34, 11-16.

Beinart, P. (1999, February 15). Private matters. *The New Republic.* 21-25.

Belz, J. (1994, July). *A brief history of World magazine and God's World Publications, Inc.* Asheville, NC: God's World Publications.

A big row is on. Capital to be continued as 'Christian daily.' Business manager Keizer says it shall not be. Mr. popenoe is firm. Holds a majority of the stock in his name. Four directors out of vie approve the plan. Gen. Hudson may quit. Says he will never edit any but secular daily, must be partisan Republican in politics. (1900, March 17). *Topeka State Journal,* p. 1.

Blanchard, M.A. (1996). Freedom of the press, 1690-1804. In W. D. Sloan, and J. D. Startt, (Eds.), *The media in America, a history.* (pp. 121-152). Northport, AL: Vision Press.

Bleyer, W. G. (1927). *A history of American journalism.* Boston: Houghton Mifflin.

Bohlander, R. (1992). Vol. 1, *The Progressive Era and the First World War (1900-1918)*. McMillan Publishing: New York.

Boorstin, D.J. (1973). *The Americans: The democratic experience*. New York: Random House.

Bordwell, D. (1989). *Making meaning, inference and rhetoric in the interpretation of cinema*. Cambridge: Harvard University Press.

Bormann, E. G. (1972). Fantasy and rhetorical vision: The rhethorical criticism of social reality. *Quarterly Journal of Speech, 58*, 396-407.

Bormann, E. G. (1973). The Eagleton affair: A fantasy theme analysis. *Quarterly Journal of Speech, 59*, 143-159.

Bormann, E. G. (1976). General and specific theories of communication. In J.E. Golden, G.F. Berquist, & W. E. Coleman (Eds.), *The rhetoric of western thought* (pp. 431-449). Dubuque, IA: Kendal/Hunt.

Bormann, E. G. (1982). A fantasy theme analysis of the television coverage of the hostage release and the Reagan Inaugural. *Quarterly Journal of Speech, 68,* 133-145.

Bormann, E. G. (1983). Symbolic convergence: Organizational communication and culture. In L.L. Putnam & M.E. Pacanowsky (Eds.), *Communication and organizations: An interpretive approach*. Newbury Park, CA: Sage.

Bormann, E. G. (1985). Symbolic convergence theory: a communication formulation. *Journal of Communication, 5,* (35), 128-138.

Bormann, E. G. (2000). Fantasy and rhetorical vision: The rhetorical criticism of social reality. In C. Burgchardt (Ed.), *Readings in rhetorical criticism* (pp. 248-259). State College, PA: Strata.

Bright, J. (1900, March 13). Is the war just? *The Topeka Daily Capital*, p. 1.

Buddenbaum, J. M. (1987, Summer/Autumn). "Judge . . . What their acts will justify:" The religion journalism of James Gordon Bennett. *Journalism History, 14*, 2-3.

Butterfield, H. (1931). *The Whig interpretation of history.* London: Bell and Sons.

Cairns, E. E. (1979). *God and man in time, A Christian approach to historiography*. Grand Rapids, MI: Baker Book House.

Carey, J. W. (1989). *Communication as culture: Essay on media and society*. Boston: Unwin Hyman.

Carey, J. W. (1974). The problem of journalism history. *Journalism History, 1* (1), 3 5, 27.

Chase, H. T. (1900, March 14). Funds for India. *The Topeka Daily Capital*, p. 1.

The Christian daily. (1900, February 6). *The Topeka Daily Capital,* p. 1.

Clark, C.E. (1991). Boston and the nurturing of newspapers: Dimensions of the cradle, 1690-1741. *New England Quarterly, 2* (64), 243-271.

Colton, J. G. (1968). *Twentieth century.* Time-Life Books: New YorkBarb

Connors, T. D. (1982). *Dictionary of mass media and communication.* New York: Longman.

Copeland, D. (1995, September). *The Presence of God Was Much Seen in Their Assemblies: Religious News in Colonial America.* American Journalism Historians Association, Tulsa,Okla..

Covert, C. L. (1981, Spring). Journalism history and women's experience: A problem in conceptual change. *Journalism History, 8* (1), 2-6.

Crafts, W. F. (1900, March 14). Sunday observance. *The Topeka Daily Capital,* p. 1.

Cressy, D. (1987). *Coming over: Migration and communication between England and New England in the seventeenth century.* New York: Cambridge University Press.

Daniel, C. (1987). *Chronicle of the twentieth century.* Mount Kisco, New York: Chronicle Publications

Danner, W. M. (1900, March 13). Colorado's burden. *The Topeka Daily Capital,* p. 1.

Declines to talk. (1900, March 20). *The Topeka Daily Capital,* p. 5.

Delp, R. W. (1985). The southern press and the rise of American spiritualism, 1847 1860. *Journal of American Culture, 7* (3), 88-95.

Dicken-Garcia, H. (1989). *Journalistic standards in nineteenth-century America.* University of Wisconsin Press: Madison, WI.

Dougall, J.R. (1900, March 17). A Christian daily. *The Topeka Daily Capital,* p. 1.

Ek, R. (1974, Spring). The irony of Sheldon's newspaper." *Journalism Quarterly, 51.* 1: 22-27.

Eisenstein, E. (1995). The rise of the reading public. In D. Crowley, D. & P.Heyer, (Eds.), *Communication in history, technology, culture, society* (pp. 105-113). New York: Longman.

Emery, M., Emery, E., and Roberts, N. L. (1996). *The press and America, An interpretive history of the mass media* (8th ed.). Englewood Cliffs, NJ: Prentice Hall.

Everett, G. (1996). The age of new journalism, 1883-1900. In W. D. Sloan and J. D. Startt (Eds.), *The media in America, A history* (pp. 275-304). Northport, AL: Vision Press.

A fair suffrage. (1900, March 15). *The Topeka Daily Capital,* p. 1.

Ferre, J. P. (1988). *A Social Gospel for millions: the religious bestsellers of Charles Sheldon, Charles Gordon, Harold Bell Wright.* Bowling Green, OH: Bowling Green State University Popular Press.

A final word as to the Sheldon paper. (1900, March 28). *The Topeka Daily Capital*, p. 4.

Folkerts, J., Tetter Jr., D. L. (1989). *Voices of a nation, a history of media in the United States.* New York: Macmillan Publishing Co.

For the sake of humanity. (1900, March 14). *The Topeka Daily Capital*, p. 1.

Foss, S. K. (1996). *Rhetorical criticism, exploration and practice* (2nd ed.). Prospect Heights, IL: Waveland.

Francke, W. (1985, Winter-Autumn). Sensationalism and the development of nineteenth-century reporting: The broom sweeps sensory details. *Journalism History, (12),* 80-85.

From Gov. Stanley. (1900, January 23). *The Topeka Daily Capital*, p. 2.

Gottschalk, L. R. (1950). *Understanding history.* New York: Alfred A. Knopf.

Grady, J. L. (1991, November). Journalism and the Gospel. Providential Perspective, *The Monthly Journal of The Providence Foundation*, Charlottesville, VA, 6 (7), 1-6.

Greater Topeka, The men whose personal property raises the funds to run the machinery of local and state government. (1900, March 19). *Topeka State Journal*, p. 1.

Grenz, S. J. and Olson, R. E. (1992). *Twenieth-century theology, God and the world in a transitional age.* Downers Grove, IL: InterVarsity Press.

Geertz, C. (1973). Thick description: Toward an interpretive theory of culture in *The interpretation of cultures.* New York: Basic Books, p. 5.

Griffin, E. (1997). *Communication, A first look at communication theory.* New York: McGraw-Hill.

Hackett, A. P. (1976). *70 years of best sellers.* New York: R. R. Bowker Co.

Hart, B. (1987). *Faith and freedom. The Christian roots of American liberty.* Dallas, TX: Lewis and Stanley.

Hart, R. P. (1990). *Modern rhetorical criticism.* Glenview, IL: Scott, Foresman/Little, Brown Higher Education.

Harvey, H. (1989). *The condition of postmodernity.* Cambridge: Basil Blackwell.

Hastings, J. (1919). *Encyclopedia of religion and ethics.* New York: Charles Scribner's Sons.

Henry, S. (1976). Colonial woman printer as prototype: Toward a model for the study of minorities. *Journalism History, 3* (1), 20-24.

Hensley, C. W. (1975). Rhetorical vision and the persuasion of a historical movement: The Disciples of Christ in nineteenth century American culture, *Quarterly Journal of Speech, 61*, 250-264.

Hoffert, S. D. (1993). New York City's Penny Press and the issue of woman's rights, 1848-1860. *Journalism Quarterly, 70,* (3), 656-665.

Hollis, D. W. III. (1995). *The ABC-CLIO companion to the media in America.* Santa Barbara, CA: ABC-CLIO.

Houston, H. S. (1936, June 27). Truth drive began in the early days. *Editor and Publisher*, pp. 15-16.

Hoover, S. M. (1998). *Religion in the news, Faith and journalism in American public discourse.* London: Sage Publications.

How the savior would conduct a modern newspaper. (1900, February 6). *The Topeka Daily Capital*, p. 6.

Howard, C. N. (1900, March 13). The cry for work. *The Topeka Daily Capital*, p. 1.

Hudson, J. K. (1900, February 6). By Gen. J.K. Hudson, editor of *The Topeka Daily Capital. The Topeka Daily Capital*, p. 6.

Hoover, S. M. and Radelfinger, M. (1989, October). *The RNS-Lilly Study of Religion Reporting and Readership in the Daily Press.* Philadelphia: Temple University.

Hudson, F. (1968). *Journalism in the United States from 1690-1872).* New York: NY: Hashee House Publishers Ltds., Publishers of Scare Scholarly Books.

Hutchinson, M. (1998, November 16). It's a small church after all. *Christianity Today, 42* (13), 45-52.

Jaki, S. L. (1993, Fall). History as science and science in history. *The Intercollegiate Review*, 11-19.

Jenkins, D. (1987). Congregationalism. In E. Mircea (Ed.), *The encyclopedia of religion, Vol. 4* (pp. 42-45). New York: Macmillan Publishing Co.

Jones, H. M. (1971). *The age of energy: varieties of American experience, 1865-1915.* New York: Viking Press.

Keeler, J.D., Tarpley, J.D.; and Smith, M.R.. (2000). The National Coruier, news, religious ideology. In W.D. Sloan, (Ed.), *Media and religion in American history.* Northport, AL: Vision Press.

Kielbowicz, R.B. (1996). The media and reform, 1900-1917. In W. D. Sloan and J.D. Startt, (Eds.), *The media in America, A history.* (pp. 365-384). Northport, AL: Vision Press.

Knowlton, S. R. and Parsons, P. R. (1993). *The journalist's moral compass: Basic principles.* Westport, CT: Greenwood Publishing Group, Inc.

Kobre, S. (1969). *Development of American Journalism.* Dubuque, IA: William C. Brown.

Lee, A. M. (1937). *The daily newspaper in America, The evolution of a social instrument.* New York: MacMillan.

Lee, J. M. (1917). *A history of American journalism.* Garden City, NY: The Garden City Publishing Co.

Littlejohn, S. W. (1992). *Theories of human communication, 5th edition.* Belmont, California: Wadsworth Publishing Co.

Licther, S.R., Lichter, L.S., Rothman, S. (1986). *The media elite.* Bethesda, MD: Adler and Adler.

Lo Bello, N. (1989). When Christ was editor in Kansas. *Media History Digest, 9*,1, (Spring, Summer): 2-5, 30-31.

Lo Bello, N. (1985, February).When Christ was editor in Kansas. *MD Magazine*: pp. 50-55.

Magill, F. N. (1980). *Great Events from History, Worldwide Twentieth Century Series Vol. I,* 1900-1940. Salem Press: Englewood, N. J.

Mander, M. (1982, Spring). Pen and sword: Problems of reporting the Spanish American War. *Journalism History, 1* (9), 2-9.

Marsden, G. M. (1994). *The soul of the American university. From protestant establishment to established nonbelief.* New York: Oxford.

McCormick, R. L. (1990). *Public life in industrial America in E. Froner. The New American History.* Philadelphia: Temple University Press.

McKerns, J. P. (1977, Autumn). The limits of progressive journalism history. *Journalism History, 4* (3), 88-92.

Mencher, M. (1999). *Basic media writing.* (6th ed.). Boston: McGraw-Hill College.

Miller, T. (1987). *Following In his steps, a biography of Charles M. Sheldon.* Knoxville: The University of Tennessee Press.

Mott, F. L. (1941). *American journalism, a history of newspapers in the United States through 250 years, 1690 to 1940.* New York: The Macmillan Co.

Mott, F. L. (1947). *Golden multitudes, The story of best sellers in the United States.* New York: R. R. Bowker Co.

Moyer, E. and Cairns, E. E. (1982*). Wycliffe biographical dictionary of the church.* Chicago: Moody Press.

Nelson, J. W. (1976). *Your God is alive and well and appearing in popular culture.* Philadelphia: Westminster.

Nerone, J.C. (1989). *The culture of the press in the early republic, Cincinnati, 1793-1848.* New York: Garland Publishing.

Nerone, J. C. (1987). The mythology of the penny press. *Critical Studies in Mass Communication, 4,* 376-404.

Neuhaus, R. J. (1984). *The naked public square, religion and democracy in America. (2nd. ed.).* Grand Rapids, MI: William B. Eerdmans Publishing Co.

New opportunities in old professions: An address given at Washburn College commencement, Topeka, Kansas, June 14, 1899. (1899). Chicago: J. A. Ulrich.

Noll, M. A. (1996). *A history of Christianity in the United States and Canada.* Grand Rapids, MI: William B. Eerdmans Publishing Co.

Nord, D. P. (1984, March). The evangelical origins of mass media in America, 1815-1835. *Journalism Monograph, Association for Education in Journalism and Mass Communication.*

Nord, D. P. (1990, June). Teleology and the news: The religious roots of American journalism, 1630-1730. *The Journal of American History, 77* (2), 9-38.

Olasky, M. (1991). *Central ideas in the development of American journalism: A narrative history.* Hillsdale: Lawrence Erlbaum Associates.

Olasky, M. (1988). *Prodigal press, The anti-Christian bias of the American news media.* Westchester, IL: Crossway Books.

Olasky, M. (1996). *Telling the truth.* Wheaton, IL: Crossways.

Over 20,000,000 readers. (1900, January 23). *The Topeka Daily Capital,* p. 7.

Payne, G. N. (1920). *History of journalism in the United States.* New York: D. Appleton and Co.

Pratte, A. (1993, June 4-6). *The media as a church.* Paper presented at Regent University conference on Faith, Story and Community.

Press of the nation on Sheldon idea. (1900, February 11). *The Topeka Daily Capital,* p. 10.

Prohibition tested. (1900, March 13). *The Topeka Daily Capital,* p. 1.

Puente, M. (1999, February 24). The century's biggest news. *USA Today,* pp. D1-2.

Rauschenbusch, W. (1912). Christianizing the social order. New York: Macmillan.

Rev. Charles M. Sheldon to edit the capital. (1900, January 23). *The Topeka Daily Capital,* p. 1.

Rev. Mr. Sheldon's sermon. (1900, March 20). *The Topeka Daily Capital,* p. 5.

Rice, C. L. (1987). *Preaching. In E. Mircea (Ed.), The encyclopedia of religion, Vol. 11* (pp. 494-497). New York: Macmillan Publishing Co.

Ripley, J. W. (1965, Spring). Another look at the Rev. Mr. Charles M. Sheldon's Christian daily newspaper. *The Kansas Historical Quarterly, 31* (1).

Ripley, J. W. (1968, Fall). The strange story of Charles M. Sheldon's *In his steps. The Kansas Historical Quarterly, 34* (1).

Riley, S. G. (1996). American magazines, 1740-1900. In W.D. Sloan and J. D. Startt, (Eds.), *The media in America, A history* (pp. 305-320). Northport, AL: Vision Press.

Rosen, J. (1996). *Getting the connections right, public journalism and the troubles in the press.* New York: The Twentieth Century Fund Press.

Sanctified sacrilege. (1900, March 21). *The New York Daily Tribune,* p. 3.

Schiller, D. (1981). *Objectivity and the news. The public and the rise of commercial journalism.* Philadelphia: University of Pennsylvania Press.

Schudson, M. (1978). *Discovering the news. A social history of American newspapers.* New York: Basic Books.

Schudson, M. (1987). Critical response: A revolution in historiography? *Critical Studies in Mass Communication, 4,* 405-408.

Shaw, D. L. and Slater, J. W. (1985, Winter-Autumn). In the eye of the beholder? Sensationalism in American press news, 1820-1860. *Journalism History, 3-4,* (12), 86 -91.

Sheldon, C. M. (1900a, March 16). Against war. *The Topeka Daily Capital,* p. 1.

Sheldon, C. M. (1925). *Charles M. Sheldon, his life story.* New York: George H. Doran Co.

Sheldon, C. M. (1900b, March 14). The cost of crime. *The Topeka Daily Capital,* p. 1.

Sheldon, C. M. (1900). *The first Christian daily paper and other sketches.* New York: Street and Smith.

Sheldon, C. M. (1900c, March 17 morning). Four open letters. *The Topeka Daily Capital,* p. 2.

Sheldon, C. M. (1900d, March 17 morning). Funeral customs. *The Topeka Daily Capital,* p. 1.

Sheldon, C. M. (1994). *In his steps.* Grand Rapids, MI: Fleming H. Revell.

Sheldon, C. M. (1900e, March 17 morning). Is the world ready for a Christian daily? *The Topeka Daily Capital,* p. 1.

Sheldon, C. M. (1900f, March 16). Moral issues. *The Topeka Daily Capital*, p. 2.

Sheldon, C. M. (1900g, March 17 morning). Newspaper advertising. *The Topeka Daily Capital*, p. 1.

Sheldon, C. M. (1900h, March 16). Social settlement. *The Topeka Daily Capital*, p. 1.

Sheldon, C. M. (1900i, March 13). Starving India. *The Topeka Daily Capital*, p. 1.

Sheldon, C. M. (1900j, March 17 evening). The Saturday evening edition. *The Topeka Daily Capital*, p. 2

Sheldon, C. M. (1900n, March 13, 1900). Starving India. *The Topeka Daily Capital*, p. 1.

Sheldon, C. M. (1900k, March 14). The tax dodger. *The Topeka Daily Capital*, p. 1.

Sheldon, C. M. (1900l, March 13). The Topeka Capital this week. *The Topeka Daily Capital*, p. 2

Sheldon, C. M. (1900m, March 15). The union of Christendom. *The Topeka Daily Capital*, p. 1.

Sheldon, C. M. (1900o, March 15). Use of tobacco. *The Topeka Daily Capital*, p. 1.

Sheldon, C. M. (1900r, March 14). What can we do to make this a better city. *The Topeka Daily Capital*, p. 2.

Sheldon, C. M. (1900s, March 15). The world's greatest need. *The Topeka Daily Capital*, p. 2.

The Sheldon edition. (1900, March 25). *The Topeka Daily Capital*, p. 9.

Sheldon edition, Editorial comments from papers East and West, Various opinions given, Some do not like scheme of mixing editorials and news–views in general. (1900, March 20). *The Topeka Daily Capital*, p. 6.

Sheldon edition, Editorial comments from papers East and West, What some of the Chicago ministers have to say of the experiment. (1900, March 21). *The Topeka Daily Capital*, p. 6.

The Sheldon edition of the Capital. (1900, March 20). *The Topeka Daily Capital*, p. 4

The Sheldon edition, What ministers, religious papers and the daily press say of it. (1900, March 25). *The Topeka Daily Capital*, p. 9.

Sheldon issue endorsed. (1900, March 21). *The Topeka Daily Capital*, p. 8.

Sheldon Week. (1900, March 20). *The Topeka Daily Capital*, p. 6.

Shelley, B. L. (1996). *Church history in plain language*. Dallas, TX: Word.

Silk, M. (1995). *Unsecular media, Making news of religion in America.* Chicago: University of Illinois Press.

Sloan, W. D. and Startt, J. D. (1996). *The media in America, a history.* Northport, Ala.: Vision Press.

Sloan, W.D. (1991). The New England Courant: Voice of Anglicanism, the role religion in colonial journalism. *American Journalism, 8,* (2/3), 106-141.

Sloan, W. D. (1987). The party press and the freedom of the press, 1798-1888. *American Journalism, 4* (2), 82-96.

Sloan, W. D. (1991). *Perspectives on mass communication history.* Hillsdale, N.J.: Lawrence Erlbaum Associates.

Sloan, W.D. and Startt, J. D. (1996). *The media in America, a history.* Norport, AL: Vision Press.

Sloan, W.D. (1993, Summer-Fall). Why study history? *American Journalism, 10,* (3 4), 6-10.

Smith, M. R. (1998, January 10). The Jesus bracelet fad: Is it merchandising or ministry? *World,* p. 17.

Smith, M. R. (1990, February 10). Ownership changes. *Editor & Publisher,* p. 29.

Smith, M. R. (1992, May 30). Small-town upheaval. *Editor & Publisher,* 9-10.

Stanley, W. E. (1900, March 14). Prison reform. *The Topeka Daily Capital,* p. 1.

Startt, J. (1993, Summer-Fall). Historiography and the media historian. *American Journalism, 10* (3-4), 17-25.

Startt, J. D. and Sloan, W. D. (1989). *Historical methods in mass communication.* Hillsdale, NJ: Lawrence Erlbaum Associates.

Stephens, M. (1997). *A history of news.* Fort Worth, TX: Harcourt Brace College Publishers.

Tarpley, J.D. (1984). Anne O'Hare McCormick. In *American Newspaper Journalists, 1926-1950.* (pp. 194-199). Detroit: Bruccoli Clark.

These are skeptical. (1900, January 25). *The Topeka Daily Capital,* p. 1.

Thomas, H. (1900, March 13). The war spirit. *The Topeka Daily Capital,* p. 1.

Thompson, K. (1988). *Breaking the glass armor: Neoformalist film analysis.* Princeton: Princeton University Press.

Toynbee, A. J. (1948). *A study of history.* London: Oxford

Toynbee, A. J. (1956). *A historian's approach to religion.* New York: Oxford University Press.

Unique idea in the history of journalism. (1900, January 23). *The Topeka Daily Capital,* p. 1.

Veith, Jr., G. E. (1994). *Postmodern times, A Christian guide to contemporary thought and culture.* Wheaton, IL: Crossway.

Waugh, P. (1992). *Postmodernism: A reader.* London: Edward Arnold.

Weber, M. (1930). *The Protestant ethic and the spirit of capitalism.* T. Parsons (Ed.) London: George Allen and Unwin. (Original work published in 1904-5). Illinois University.

Wetterau, B. (1990). *The New York Public Library Book of Chronologies.* Prentice Hall Press: New York.

Wiebe, R. H. (1967). *The search for order.* New York: Hill and Wang.

What is news? Sheldon, C. M. (1900, March 17 morning). *The Topeka Daily Capital,* p. 1.

Williams, J. H. (1994). *The media and the personification of society.* In J. D. Starr and W. D. Sloan (Eds.), The significance of the media in American history. Northport, AL: Vision Press.

Williams, N. (1966). *Chronology of the Modern World, 1763 to the present time.* David McKay Company: New York.

Williams, R. (1995). Dream worlds of consumption. In D. Crowley, D. and P. Heyer, *Communication in history, technology, culture, society.* Longman: New York.

Woodworth, R. L. (1983). *The life and writings of Charles M. Sheldon (1857-1946), with special reference to his relations with the press.* Unpublished doctoral dissertation, Southern Illinois University at Carbondale.

Index

U

V

W

Y

About the Author

Michael R. Smith

Michael R. Smith, Ph.D., is an associate professor and chair of School of Journalism at Regent University. An award-winning writer and photojournalist, Michael Smith has written more than 2,500 articles. In addition to his more than thirteen years of experience as an educator, he has worked for more than ten years in newspaper reporting and editing, where he covered general assignments, politics, and religion. His freelance articles have been published in the *Philadelphia Inquirer*, *USA Today*, the *Baltimore Sun*, the *Atlanta Constitution*, and other periodicals. He is the author of two books of local history and has published several chapters on mass media and a number of academic journal articles. A member of *Who's Who Among American Teachers* and *Who's Who in Communication*, Michael conducts research on Christianity and mass media and is a frequent speaker at writer's conferences.